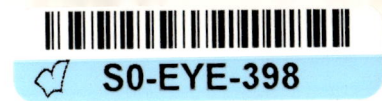

# Using Reading to Teach Subject Matter

## Fundamentals for Content Teachers

Arnold Burron
*University of Northern Colorado*

Amos L. Claybaugh
*University of Northern Colorado*

CHARLES E. MERRILL PUBLISHING COMPANY
*A Bell & Howell Company*  Columbus, Ohio  43216

*The Charles E. Merrill*
**COMPREHENSIVE READING PROGRAM**

**Arthur W. Heilman**
**Consulting Editor**

Published by
CHARLES E. MERRILL PUBLISHING COMPANY
*A Bell & Howell Company*
Columbus, Ohio 43216

Copyright © 1974 by Bell & Howell Company. All rights reserved. No part of this book may be reproduced in an any form, electronic or mechanical, including photocopy, recording, or any information storage or retrieval system, without permission in writing from the publisher.

Library of Congress Catalog Card Number: 73-90572

International Standard Book Number: 0-675-08838-0

5 6 6 7 8 9 10—78

PRINTED IN THE UNITED STATES OF AMERICA

# Preface

There are many ways in which the teaching of reading can be approached. Machines, worksheets, games, kits, skill exercises, teacher-participation activities, carefully structured programs, systems approaches, and other avenues have all been utilized in making a contribution to children's growth in reading. But too frequently, though, reading is thought of only as another subject to be taught—one which commands an important and substantial part of the school day, but one which is, nevertheless, taught during a specified time period as a special subject, with little carry-over into other academic areas where the application of reading skills is both desirable and necessary.

It is the purpose of this book to show subject-matter teachers how information relative to reading instruction can make an important contribution to the teaching of subject-matter courses and to illustrate how, in the process of applying information, procedures, and techniques commonly applied in "reading" classes, teachers can increase the achievement of their students in the subject-matter fields. Hence, the title of the book is an accurate description of its contents; the emphasis of the book has been placed on achieving more productive teaching of subject matter through the application of a few basic ideas in reading rather than on teaching reading through the subject-matter fields. The authors believe that subject-matter teachers are primarily interested in teaching subject matter—and understandably so. This belief is the reason for the emphasis which was chosen.

Throughout the chapters which follow, the attempt has been made to avoid the use of specialized terminology and a formal style of writing which is usually evident in a textbook. If the reader infers that this is a book which was written for generalists in self-contained classrooms or content area specialists in open-space or departmentalized schools rather than for "reading" teachers and that the content is so basic that it can be applied "tomorrow" by even a relatively inexperienced student-teacher or a subject-matter teacher whose field is not the field of reading, then the purpose of this book has been accomplished.

**Arnold Burron**
**Amos L. Claybaugh**

# Acknowledgements

We wish to express our appreciation to Dr. Adolph Christenson, Reading Consultant, Spokane, Washington Public Schools, whose helpful suggestions aided in the preparation of this book. The authors are grateful for his assistance.

We also gratefully acknowledge permission to reprint "The Cone of Experience" from *Audiovisual Methods in Teaching*, 3rd ed. by Egar Dale (Hinsdale, Illinois: The Dryden Press, 1969), by permission of the publisher. Copyright © 1969 by The Dryden Press, Inc.

# Contents

| | | |
|---|---|---|
| Introduction | What Should Be Taught by the Subject-Matter Teacher? | 1 |
| Chapter One | Common Reading Problems Found in Subject-Matter Materials | 9 |
| Chapter Two | Skills Necessary for Reading Subject-Matter Material | 21 |
| Chapter Three | Identifying Reading Strengths and Weaknesses of the Subject-Matter Student | 37 |
| Chapter Four | Evaluating the Textbook and Utilizing Reference Sources | 59 |
| Chapter Five | Capitilizing on Knowledge of Students and Materials | 69 |
| Chapter Six | Using Instructional Time Effectively | 85 |
| Chapter Seven | Utilizing Other Learning Aids | 99 |
| Appendix A | Answers to "A Subject-Matter Test" | 109 |

| Appendix B | Types of Word Pronunciation Errors: The IRI | 113 |
| Appendix C | Source for Media Materials | 115 |
| Appendix D | Suggested Readings | 117 |
| Index | | 119 |

*INTRODUCTION*

# What Should Be Taught by the Subject-Matter Teacher?

"Why on earth do they want us to attend an in-service session in teaching *reading?*" The preceding statement is an example of the kind of sentiment forcefully expressed by subject-matter teachers who are asked to participate in sessions devoted to the teaching of reading in the content fields. The exclamation above is actually a mild example of what is really said. Often, a negative attitude is asserted much more vigorously, couched in a manner which allows for the liberal interjection of appropriate expletives, and it is accompanied by a barrage of additional questions which are asked more for the purpose of demonstrating incredulity than for the purpose of seeking answers, such as:

"Is instruction in reading *really* related to effective teaching of subject matter?"

"Is it absolutely necessary that I be as concerned about teaching reading skills as I am about teaching science (mathematics, history, industrial arts, etc.)?"

"How can reading skills for subject matter be as important to achievement in my subject as the facts or concepts which constitute the *content* of my subject?"

## 2    What Should Be Taught by the Subject-Matter Teacher?

In an attempt to provide partial answers to these questions, the participation of teachers in answering the items on the short quiz which follows is often solicited. The items included in the quiz are representative of facts, concepts, or key ideas taught in subject-matter courses. Most of the teachers learned these facts, concepts, or key ideas in classes such as general science, English, industrial arts or home economics, social studies, and mathematics. You may wish to try the quiz yourself, and then, based on your self-evaluation of your achievement on the quiz, attempt to answer the three questions on page 1 on your own.

### A SUBJECT-MATTER TEST

1. A. You have decided to buy some fruit trees for a building site you've purchased. However, you have room for only two trees. You'd like an apple tree and a peach tree, but you don't know whether the apple tree can pollinate the peach tree, or vice versa, and there are no other fruit trees in the neighborhood. To ensure a harvest of fruit, would you:

    1) buy two apple trees, so pollination can take place?
    2) buy two peach trees, so pollination can take place?
    3) buy one tree of each kind and assume that each tree will self-pollinate, or assume that each tree will pollinate the other tree?

   B. What type of printed source would tell you the answer to #1A?

   C. Assuming that you identified a source, under what entry would you look?

2. A. The building site you've bought includes access to an irrigation ditch. You need to water your trees (if you ever decide what kinds of trees to buy), and the ditch is the only source of water for the purpose of watering your site. You are allowed to install a water pump. What kind of a water pump would you install to pump water from the ditch?

   B. What agencies could provide printed sources to tell you the answer to #2A?

   C. Assuming that you identified a source, under what entry would you look?

# What Should Be Taught by the Subject-Matter Teacher? 3

3. A. A friend of yours, on learning of the site you've purchased, exclaims, "Did you know that there is bentonite out there!" You are:

   1) concerned, because you don't own the mineral rights to the property, and you're afraid a mining company will move in soon;
   2) concerned, because bentonite will limit you in designing your new home;
   3) unconcerned, because bentonite, you seem to remember from your class in physical science, is the scientific name for the layer of soil found under the subsoil.

   B. What readily available printed source would tell you the answer to #3A? _____

4. A. You can remember learning all about similes, metaphors, and other such concepts in English class, and you can usually readily understand figurative language, but now you've been asked to explain the following:

   > Remember now thy Creator in the days of thy youth, while the evil days come not, or the years draw nigh, when thou shalt say, "I have no pleasure in them.". . . In the day when the keepers of the house shall tremble, and the strong men shall bow themselves, and the grinders cease because they are few, and those that look out of the windows be darkened. And the doors shall be shut in the streets. . . and he shall rise up at the voice of the bird. . .

   Explain what the selection means: _____

   B. You know the selection is from the Bible, but you don't know from which book it has been taken. Where would you look to find the answer?

   C. Have parts of the selection been omitted? _____ How do you know? _____

   D. Is there a printed source which can be used to explain the selection to you? _____

   E. If yes, what would the source be? _____

5. A. You can remember learning about the AFL-CIO somewhere in a history

**4    What Should Be Taught by the Subject-Matter Teacher?**

        class, and a part of what you learned had to do with the impact of the AFL–CIO on American society. What is the AFL–CIO? _____

    B. ("An organization" is not a sufficient answer). Suppose you know only that it is an organization. What printed source would quickly tell you the name of this and other similar organizations? _____

    C. What commonly available printed source would tell you the address of the headquarters of the AFL–CIO in the event that you wanted to write to this organization? _____

6. A. It has been suggested that Vitamin C in large quantities can be taken to preclude a person's succumbing to the common cold. It has also been suggested that Vitamin C in large quantities could be harmful. Write down all you can remember from your science, health, or home ec. classes about Vitamin C. _____

    B. If you can't remember much about Vitamin C, what printed source, other than a science or health textbook, could be used to find the information? _____

7. A. A wealthy uncle has agreed to loan you $2400 for 36 months at 5 3/4 percent annual interest on the unpaid balance. How much interest would you pay the first month, assuming that your payments are $100 per month? _____

    B. Suppose you paid the loan off in 24 months, and you wanted to refigure the interest payments, since you had originally figured the interest on the basis of 36 months. Your uncle says the interest paid would be the same. Is he right? _____

    C. What would be a good source to consult to make sure that no overpayment or underpayment of interest occurs? _____

8. A. What is a "filister head" machine screw? _____

    B. What would be a good printed source which would provide the answer? _____

9. A. What is a French seam? _____

# What Should Be Taught by the Subject-Matter Teacher? 5

What is the advantage of using the French seam instead of a regular stitched seam? _____

B. What type of printed source would show you how to sew various types of seams? _____

10. A. A radio quiz show announcer just called you on the telephone. The question he has asked you—which you have one minute to answer—is, "Farmers in Canada's prairie provinces know much about rape. To a farmer in Canada, what is the first definition of rape which crosses his mind in the fall of the year?" Previous answers, such as "forced gratification," "plunder," and related ideas have been wrong. The announcer tells you that rape is an agricultural product grown in Canada's prairie provinces. A social studies book is near the phone. You naturally remember that one of Canada's prairie provinces is _____

B. Now you look up "rape" in the social studies book, by checking what part of the book? _____

What entries would you use? _____

C. Once you've located "rape," you find the following:

rape, 39, 78, 123–125, 126p.

Underline the page(s) you'd turn to.

11. A. The reading study skills of evaluation and organization can be applied to this quiz. Test yourself. For each question, identify the subject-matter area from which each question might have been derived (e.g., Would question #1 come from an English class, a science class, or. . .?) ___

_____

B. Can you identify the major purpose of this quiz? _____

C. If a major purpose is not readily apparent to you, perhaps the application of the reading study skill of "organization" will help you get the answer to 11B. Can you organize this quiz into two categories or types of questions? For example, which questions can be categorized as "fact" questions, eliciting responses related to content which you were probably taught at one time or another during your public school experience? ___

_____

## 6   What Should Be Taught by the Subject-Matter Teacher?

Which questions are "study skill" or process-oriented questions which could be legitimately taught in any content area? _____

Now try #11B if you missed it earlier.*

If your experience in attempting the quiz was similar to that of most graduate students who took the quiz in the past, you probably discovered that:

1. The quiz is really an assessment of two kinds of abilities. The first part of each question elicits solely the ability to recall or to both recall and apply specific facts or concepts from a subject-matter field. The second, and in some cases, the third part of each item elicits the ability to apply knowledge of a reading study skill.
2. You probably achieved greater success on the parts of the items related to reading study skills than you did on the parts of the items related to recall of specific content. In either case, however, your achievement was probably not better than 50 percent accuracy. Achievement of less than 30 percent accuracy on this quiz is quite typical of the achievement of teachers from numerous states in the country. (Questions 1A and 4A have been answered correctly by only 2 percent of teachers who have taken the quiz.)

In considering the information that there are two main kinds of subject-matter learnings represented on the test—the learning of specific facts or concepts and the learning of specific study skills related to the study of subject matter—which type of learning seems to have greater applicability to you in problem-solving activities related to your present life situation? Many teachers agree with the authors that knowing the skills related to finding specific information is more important than retaining specific items of information. This seems to be an especially logical conclusion when one considers the vast quantity of information which confronts the contemporary learner. If this conclusion is a tenable conclusion, it would seem equally tenable to advocate that selected reading skills be taught by the subject-matter teacher, and that discussions, activities, and assignments in subject-matter classes include student responses which call for application of these selected skills. This is not to suggest a derogation of the importance of subject-matter content. Fruitful

---
*Answers to questions 1-10 on the quiz can be found in Appendix A.

## What Should Be Taught by the Subject-Matter Teacher? 7

study is impossible without some mastery of the content the learner might encounter in situations demanding reading ability. The authors contend, however, that both content *and* concomitant reading skills are essential components of successful subject-matter teaching and learning.

The information, techniques, and procedures advocated in the pages which follow reflect an application of the philosophy discussed above; namely, that certain reading skills have direct applicability to the learning of content, that these skills can be appropriately classified as "subject-matter reading skills," that the teaching of these skills is indispensable to the effective teaching of content, and that the subject-matter teacher who is willing and able to teach selected reading skills can be a more effective teacher of subject matter.

A discussion of reading problems posed by subject-matter materials is presented in Chapter One. In Chapter Two, the reading study skills necessary for reading content materials are described. Chapter Three is devoted to an exposition of techniques for identifying students' reading strengths and weaknesses. Chapter Four suggests how textbooks can be evaluated and how reference sources can be used in content classes. Chapter Five explores approaches to individualization of instruction and an approach to making meaningful reading assignments. The effective use of instructional time is considered in Chapter Six. Chapter Seven, the final chapter, suggests the utilization of learning aids which do not require reading, for teaching subject matter when reading about subject matter is not the most appropriate avenue for learning.

*CHAPTER ONE*

# Common Reading Problems Found in Subject-Matter Materials

Teachers do not need to be presented with research evidence to be convinced that subject matter can be difficult for their students to read. When teachers "talk shop" their anecdotes provide vivid examples of problems students have in reading subject matter. For example, one teacher reported that when a sixth-grade student in her parochial school classroom was asked to write a biographical sketch of Pontius Pilate, the Roman governor who supervised the crucifixion of Christ, he responded with a verbatim copy of a sketch in a resource text followed by a note to his teacher which said: "I read everything about Pontius Pilate that I could find, but I could not find any facts about the Roman Air Force. Why would a Pilate be in charge of the army?" At another school, in response to an "open-book" test in a science class, a student provided the following answer to his teacher's question: "A look at diagram 1 and diagram 2 will tell some things about the liver. Although diagram 1 does not have a picture of the liver in it, diagram 2 does. If diagram 2 is placed over diagram 1, it looks like the liver contains part of the stomach. So the liver must have two jobs. It protects the top of the stomach. It also must help in digestion." In yet another science class, a student teacher assigned to his pupils the task of reading an expository selection on mammals, to

# 10  Common Reading Problems Found in Subject Matter

be followed by a written description of mammals. One pupil wrote: "One fact about mammals is that, except for a certain kind of duck [an obvious reference to the duckbilled platypus], their young are born alive. This must be the reason why there are more mammals around than other animals. If other animals are born dead, soon the mammals will take over."

The potential gravity of misunderstanding of subject matter is illustrated by the following answers to a test on first aid:

For fractures: "To see if the limb is broken wiggle it gently back and forth."
For asphyxiation: "Apply artificial respiration until the patient is dead."
For nosebleed: "Put the nose lower than the body."

There are many reasons for errors of the magnitude of those cited above. Even though it is true that problems in reading can be the result of a reader's limited experience, in many cases problems stem from subject-matter material itself. Certain characteristics of subject-matter writing can create difficulties for a reader. For example, the short selection which follows was intentionally written to include many of the problems faced by students when they read subject-matter. You can increase your awareness of these problems by reading the selection, studying Figures 1 and 2, and by assessing your ability to answer the questions at the end of the selection.

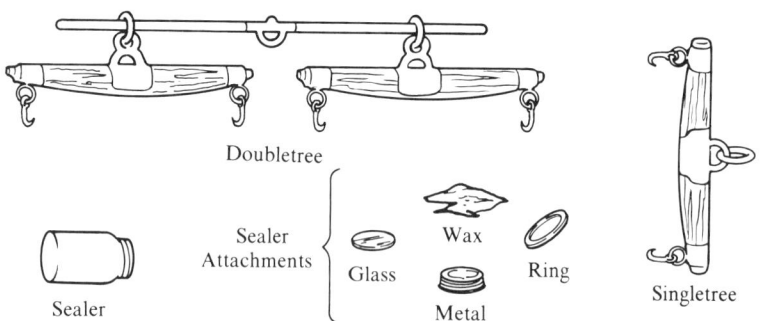

Note the similarity between the singletree and the doubletree.

**FIGURE 1**
*Functioning Anachronisms*

When is an object an anachronism? Can an object be an anachronism and a functional implement in the same geographical area? In the same time period?

## Common Reading Problems Found in Subject Matter 11

When does an object have aesthetic value? Can an object be both admired and scorned as useless in the same geographical area? In the same time period?

Does the appellation given an object reflect its value? That is, can an euphemism add value to an object (e.g., "antique" *vis-a-vis* "junk")?

Perhaps the singletree and the doubletree can provide answers. The singletree and the doubletree are like the sealer. The sealer is an anachronism. So are the singletree and the doubletree. They are also functional implements. They are anachronistic and functional in the same areas. They are anachronistic and functional in the same time period. Aesthetically, they are admired by some; aesthetically, they are disdained by others. Discrimination does not seem to be related to geographical location.

The functional decline of the singletree and the doubletree occurred before the advent of VEE.* Machine hastened their decline. Singletrees and doubletrees were not used with machines. The former were abandoned to the ravages of weather and time. Figure 2 illustrates the decline of the singletree and the doubletree as mechanized power became available. Aesthetic ascendancy of these objects is also shown.

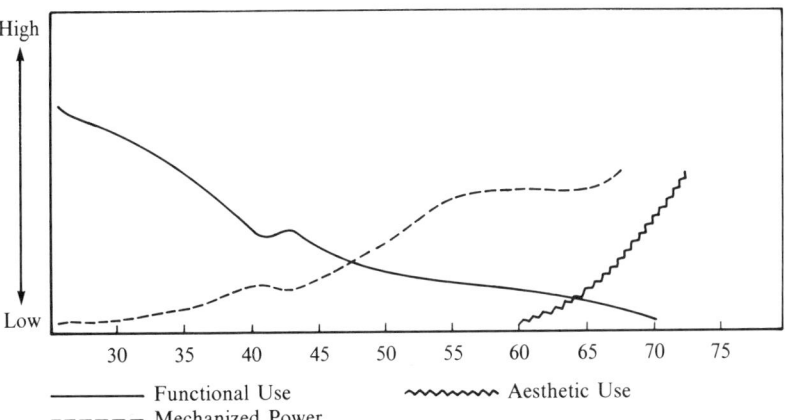

**FIGURE 2**

*Singletree-Doubletree Use*

The functional decline of the singletree and doubletree was not universal in occurrence. The aesthetic ascendancy of these objects was also

---

*Venezuelan equine encephalitis

# 12  Common Reading Problems Found in Subject Matter

not universal. In remote areas, both are used today (functionally). Some religious groups have retained them. In these areas, the sealer is also popular. However, although these objects are put to the same uses in different areas, they are called by different names in different areas. Also, where functional use in preeminent, only a modicum of aesthetic appreciation can be found.

Both the singletree and the doubletree can be made from a single tree. Metal rings or hooks are attached to the main object. The singletree is used for light loads. The doubletree is often used for heavier loads. As aesthetic objects, load is a minor factor to be considered. Here either object can be used for a single purpose. Although singletrees and doubletrees can be seen in many places, few traces of singletrees and doubletrees can be found. Weather, of course, is the reason for this.

## QUESTIONS

1. A. Why might some people incorrectly conclude that the 1971 VEE epidemic was the main cause of the decline of the popularity of the singletree and the doubletree?

   B. Why did mechanized power hasten the decline in their popularity?

2. Load is not a factor which is of major importance in discriminating between the use of a singletree and a doubletree for aesthetic purposes. Yet it is important in relation to their functional value. Why is this so?

3. How is it possible that many singletrees and doubletrees can be found, but few traces of singletrees and doubletrees can be found?

## *ANSWERS*

1. A. Singletrees are used with horses. People assumed that the deaths of large numbers of horses created a situation in which few horses were available to be hitched to singletrees.

   B. Machines were used to do much of the work formerly done by horses.

2. A doubletree is used with more than one horse when a heavy load is to be pulled. When decorative objects, such as flowerpots or beer steins, are hung from singletrees or doubletrees, the weight factor of the objects is not of significance in deciding between the use of a singletree or a doubletree.
 3. Harnesses—sometimes called "traces"—were usually made of leather and deteriorated when left outdoors for any length of time.

If you had difficulty achieving correct answers, it might be helpful to take another look at the selection in order to identify several reading problems posed by the material which may have contributed to your difficulty. The selection posed these problems:

**Background**

For lack of a more commonly used term, the designation "background" can serve as a label for a major problem posed by the selection. In numerous situations in which the selection was used by one of the authors for in-service sessions in subject-matter reading, it was discovered that without exception teachers who had had a background of experience with farm life where draft horses were used were more likely to comprehend the selection than were teachers who had no such experience. In addition, teachers who had displayed a prior interest in antiques frequently comprehended the selection. In contrast, one lifetime city-dweller, a member of the "now" generation, confidently asserted the interpretation that the selection was a treatise on forestry!

**Vocabulary**

Five distinct types of vocabulary are present in this selection as in many other content selections:

*Basic Vocabulary*: Basic vocabulary is vocabulary which describes key concepts in a selection which are fundamental to the understanding of the selection. "Singletree," "doubletree," "anachronism," "aesthetic," and "functional" are five words which constitute the basic vocabulary of the selection you read. A reader who can provide appropriate definitions for the basic vocabulary of a selection can probably achieve partial understanding even though other words might be unfamiliar to him.

*Supporting Vocabulary:* A lack of knowledge of the meanings of supporting words in a selection can detract from complete understanding of the selection. Supporting terms such as the words "euphemism," "appellation," "modicum," and "preeminent" which were used in the selection you read can be problematic for a reader.

*Multiple Meanings:* The providing of inappropriate definitions of the terms "discrimination" and "singletree" can detract from complete understanding. The most obvious example, though, of multiple meaning in the selection is presented by the word "traces." Here, failure to provide the appropriate meaning by inferring that "traces" refers to clues, instead of to harnesses, can lead the reader to a logical but completely erroneous conclusion.

*Unusual or Colloquial Terms:* Two terms, "sealer" and *vis-a-vis*, were used in the selection to clarify the key concept. In central Canada, where fruit jars are frequently referred to as "sealers," the first term would probably be readily understood. A reader with wide reading experience would readily understand the term *vis-a-vis*.

*Abbreviations:* The reader who is conversant with common abbreviations can often achieve enhanced understanding of content. In the selection, two common abbreviations, "i.e." and "e.g.," were used in one of the introductory paragraphs. A reader's awareness of an author's pointing to a clarifying phrase or supporting example by his use of abbreviations for "that is," "for example," "namely," and the like is often crucial to his understanding of a concept.

## Style

Seven rhetorical questions initiated the discussion of the singletree and the doubletree. Following the introductory paragraphs, the answer to each question was then alluded to in sequence in succeeding paragraphs. However, by the time the reader reached the seventh question, he probably had forgotten the first question. Furthermore, since the allusions to the answers appeared only after all of the questions had been posed, the reader would probably need to return to each question before reading each answer. The interrupting of reading to return to a previous portion of a selection or to study a graphic aid or other reference creates difficulties for many readers.

It does not seem necessary to point out that, in addition to the difficulties created by the series of rhetorical questions, the style of writing in the total selection you read does not lead to easy reading. Many subject-matter texts are similarly difficult to read because of the particular style in which the material is written.

## Graphic Aids

Graphic aids can often enhance understanding. They can also confuse a reader. They are often not strategically placed, and frequently they are not complete. In the selection you read, Figure 1 is not inappropriately placed, but the drawing of the singletree, vertically placed to conserve space, and with no referent to provide an indication of the size of the objects, tends to confuse rather than to clarify the concept. The horizontal drawing of the fruit jar and its attachments further tends to confuse the reader.

Seemingly minor elements omitted from the graph (Figure 2) could have a major impact on comprehension. The inclusion of the numeral "19" before each number would have been a desirable addition to indicate more clearly that the horizontal axis was a reference to years.

More complex graphic aids, containing more numerous concepts, can pose more complex and more numerous reading problems.

## Interest

Unless you are an unusually curious reader, the selection was of no interest to you, since it was written in a manner and on a topic which were chosen to lose, rather than to gain your interest. As you proceeded past the introductory paragraphs, you probably experienced apathy, frustration, or both. Much of the subject matter in a typical textbook has the same effect on students. Their needs and interests are similarly ignored. The lack of interest-inducing potential of much subject-matter material is an obvious barrier to comprehension.

The selection you read presented five main problems posed by content materials. In addition to the problems cited above, other difficulties are frequently encountered by students in their reading of subject matter.

## 16  Common Reading Problems Found in Subject Matter

Can you identify potential difficulties posed by the sample of typical fifth-grade social studies material below? How many of the problems discussed above are posed by the material? How many additional problems are posed?

### MANITOBA: THE KEYSTONE PROVINCE

MANITOBA, (MAN uh TOH buh), is one of Canada's three Prairie Provinces. Why is it called the "Keystone Province"? A look at the map on page 196 will help you decide. How long is Manitoba's southern border? The distance scale on the map of Manitoba can tell us. We can also find the distance between cities.

Find Winnipeg on the map. How far is Winnipeg from Dauphin?

The map will also give us an idea of the size of cities on the map. Is Brandon about the size of Winnipeg or about the size of Portage la Prairie? The print size will help you decide. Turn to Table 3 in the Tables of Reference. The Tables of Reference will help you check your answer.

Manitoba has over 100,000 lakes. Many of Manitoba's lakes can be found in an area called the *tundra*. Much of northern Manitoba is tundra. In what other provinces of Canada can tundra be found? Use your glossary and the map on page 197 to help you find the answer.

It is probable that the preceding passage would present the following problems for a fifth grader, as well as for students in more advanced grades.

The phonetic respelling of Manitoba could be a stumbling block. Students frequently read and reread phonetic respellings and lose continuity in their reading. Phonetic respellings can retard a student's fluency in reading and detract from understanding of what is read.

While italicized words such as the word "tundra" can be easily read, the student who does not effectively use such typographical cues can miss key concepts. In subject-matter materials, typographical cues are often presented in the form of a change from lower to upper case, a change from regular type to boldface type, a change from regular type to italics, and by the use of indentation. Each subject-matter text has a "hidden code" in the form of the kinds of typographical cues the author uses to emphasize items of varying levels of importance. A student who recognizes at once the typographical cues used to identify key ideas and supporting ideas has a distinct advantage over the student who does not have this ability.

A student who reads the "Manitoba" selection and who does not have the background to know that a keystone is the center stone in an arch will look in vain at a map of Canada, failing to see the "arch" of Canadian provinces with Manitoba at the center.

As you considered potential problems posed by the Manitoba selection, you undoubtedly identified "style" as one obvious problem. In the Manitoba selection, the reader is asked to interrupt his reading after reading only two sentences. He must look at a map, return to the selection for the question, return to the map, and then again return to the selection for directions ("find Winnipeg. . ."etc.) and another question. He might then turn again to the map, only to find that he must once again return to the selection for information and still another question. To compound his problems, he is referred to still another section of the book, the Tables of Reference, to verify answers which he probably, in his frustration, only guessed at. A quick glance at the end of the selection reveals that the reader is also directed to look at still another reference section in his book.

Several other problems posed by the style are evident in the Manitoba selection. The selection is extremely compact. Facts are presented in quick succession. Proper nouns are present in abundance. Questions are frequent. Even the author's use of punctuation can affect understanding. The sentence: "Is Brandon about the size of Winnipeg or about the size of Portage la Prairie?" could be answered with the statement, "Yes, Brandon is about the size of Winnipeg or about the size of Portage la Prairie." The simple insertion of a comma after "Winnipeg" in the question could clarify the question.

In the Manitoba selection, references to graphic aids are numerous. The student who cannot adequately read graphic aids would have a very difficult time with this selection.

The Manitoba selection does not contain an especially heavy vocabulary load, but the word "tundra" can be regarded as a potential problem because it seems to be a basic vocabulary word, the understanding of which is probably necessary to the understanding of future subject-matter reading. Many content selections present basic vocabulary words in *each* section in which a new concept is discussed.

It is probably obvious to you that the overriding problem the Manitoba selection poses for a typical fifth-grade student is the problem of interest. Yet the selection is typical of much of what can be found in content texts. Even if every other difficulty discussed above is overcome for the reader with the help provided by a skilled teacher, the problem of interest remains as perhaps the greatest concern of the subject-matter teacher.

The original list of reading problems inherent in content writing has been added to through the identification of additional barriers to compre-

## 18  Common Reading Problems Found in Subject Matter

hension present in the Manitoba selection. Other factors which are not readily identifiable in such materials can also negatively influence the achievement of success in content reading. These factors are:

1. Content materials, unlike materials in "reading" classes, are expository, not narrative. Material is presented to be retained or mastered, not necessarily to be enjoyed.

2. Higher-level reading comprehension skills are demanded. The reader must employ inferential and critical comprehension skills to a greater extent than is necessary in reading narrative materials.

3. Specialized study skills* are required for the successful study of subject matter. Advanced study skills are not often required in reading narrative materials.

## SUMMARY

A close look at a sample of what is typical of subject matter written on the level of an elementary school pupil yields a host of problems posed by the material. There is a wide variety in the kinds of obstacles to understanding encountered in the material as well as in the extent to which these obstacles affect understanding. This chapter included a discussion of the following problems posed by subject-matter materials.

1. *Background*:
   Subject-matter selections frequently assume prior knowledge and experience on the part of the student.

2. *Vocabulary*:
   Problems related to vocabulary include basic vocabulary fundamental to the understanding of key concepts in a selection, supporting vocabulary which is not included in a student's listening and speaking vocabulary, multiple meanings of words, unusual or colloquial terms, and abbreviations.

3. *Style*:
   Elements of style such as the use of rhetorical or direct questions,

---

*See Chapter Two

# Common Reading Problems Found in Subject Matter

compactness of expression, and the use of figures of speech are often found in subject-matter writing. Directions necessitating the interrupting of one's reading are common. Subject-matter writing is expository, not narrative. Material is presented to be retained, not necessarily to be enjoyed.

4. *Graphic Aids*:
   Graphic aids can be used to enhance expository writing. Often, they are included as material to be taught. A wide variety in both types of graphic aids and difficulty levels of graphic aids can be found.

5. *Interest*:
   The content of subject matter can be far removed from a student's sphere of interest.

6. *Typographical Cues*:
   The relative importance of concepts and vocabulary is often indicated through the use of typographical cues. Typographical cues include phonetic respellings, changes from upper to lower case, italics, boldface, boldface italics, and the use of indentations.

7. *Reading Comprehension Skills*:
   Advanced comprehension skills, representative of the inferential and critical levels of comprehension, are required to a greater extent in subject-matter material than in material used in "reading" classes.

8. *Reading Study Skills*:
   The reading study skills of location, evaluation, organization, and retention are required of the reader of subject matter. The reader reading for enjoyment is seldom required to employ these skills.

An awareness of the fact that content materials can create obstacles to understanding for students can lead to identification of additional obstacles to understanding which may be present in the material in use in your classroom. The ability to identify these obstacles is a good foundation upon which to build more effective subject-matter teaching abilities.

## QUESTIONS

1. Locate or write a short expository passage, appropriate in both

# 20  Common Reading Problems Found in Subject Matter

content and style for a grade level of your choice, which contains information which your pupils could not fully understand without an adequate background of experience.

2. Review the content selection below. Notice that each line in the selection is numbered. After reading the selection, list as many of the barriers to comprehension included in the list in this chapter as you can find in the selection. After each problem you list, write the number(s) of the line(s) in which the problem was encountered.

```
 1     Most cells have only one nucleus (nu´ kli es).
 2  The picture on Page 102 shows the nucleus of a cell. What
 3  is the shape of the nucleus in the picture? Notice the
 4  arrows pointing to the cytoplasm. The arrows show two
 5  particles, mitochondira (mit´ o kon´ dri e) and
 6  plastids (plas´ tidz) which are found in
 7  the cytoplasm of many cells. Plastids are not
 8  found in the human cell.
 9     Cells that work together in a group are called a
10  tissue. For example, muscle tissue is
11  a group of muscle cells. Nerve cells
12  make up nervous tissue.
13     Tissues are often grouped together to form
14  an organ. No functional
15  artificial organs have yet been made which can
16  take the place of our natural organs. Can
17  you name some organs which have been
18  successfully transplanted?
```

Difficulties posed by this material include:

1. Background, lines 16-18. (The selection assumes that the reader knows what an organ is.) _____

_____

_____

_____

_____

_____

_____

*CHAPTER TWO*

# Skills Necessary for Reading Subject-Matter Material

The process of reading is never a passive one. Regardless of the topic the writer is treating, the difficulty of vocabulary he uses, the number and kind of literal or figurative phrases he presents, or the complexity of the sentence structure he employs, the reader must be actively engaged. If not, the reader's purpose for reading will not be accomplished.

Some skills are basic to the successful reading of all printed materials. The printed word must be decoded into speech, either audibly or inaudibly, and a level of understanding must be attained in order that the purpose for reading be accomplished. Any ability or skill that is not sufficiently developed to permit a reader to decode and to comprehend will tend to hinder the person in completing the act of reading, regardless of the nature of that material.

The printed material that a student is expected to read in getting an education is commonly classified as either narrative or informative. In the early stages of learning to read, the student is usually in contact with narrative-type material. Such material capitalizes on the vocabulary and sentence structures that he is already familiar with in his oral-aural use of language. Slowly and eventually, however, his reading will be directed to more and more informative-type material, the material he is exposed to when studying subject-matter content in printed form. The skills necessary for the successful reading of informative-type materials are in addition to those generally required for reading narrative-type material. In this chapter the special skills required of a person as he attempts to purposefully read printed materials with which he is brought into contact in subject-matter courses will be presented.

## The Reading Study Skills

Skills necessary to the successful use of subject-matter material in printed form are often referred to as the Reading Study Skills. Authorities differ as to just which skills they place in this category, explaining quite satisfactorily why they include what they do include. Presented in this chapter are five skills which the authors deem necessary for adequately handling informative-type printed material usually designed for use in instruction in the subject-matter areas of the curriculum. They are:

1. *Locating* material relevant to the subject.
2. *Evaluating* the material located on the basis of its importance to the subject and its validity.
3. *Organizing* the essential information for effective use.
4. *Retaining* the needed information for its pre-determined use.
5. *Employing* a flexible rate of reading which is adjusted to the purpose for reading the material.

### The Skill of Locating Needed Information

Seldom, if ever, does a single textbook provide all the information necessary for treating a topic to be included in a subject-matter course. The student, if he is to become independent in his pursuit of a topic, will need to be efficient in locating pertinent information dealing with the topic. Such independence requires the use of a host of skills, ranging from the ability to locate information in a single volume to locating information in the varied sources in a large, well-equipped library. This section of the chapter will explore the location skills that, if mastered by the student, will enable him to be more and more independent in the location of information important to the topic he is investigating.

## Skills Necessary for Reading Subject-Matter Material 23

### Locating Information in a Single Volume

Great amounts of study time can be saved by the ability to locate relevant information efficiently in a single volume. Moving page to page through a textbook, an encyclopedia, a magazine, or even a newspaper in an attempt to locate information suggests inefficiency, especially when the information sought is specific in nature. The early application of certain location techniques can pay off in the saving of precious study time.

First, it is essential to become acquainted with the organization of the single volume in which information is being sought. Let's take a textbook for example. How is a textbook set up or organized so that information it contains can be readily located? Which of the following are likely to be of most use in locating information?

1. The Title of the Book
2. The Preface
3. The Table of Contents
4. The List of Tables
5. The List of Graphic Aids
6. The Body of the Textbook
7. The Appendixes with their varied inclusions
8. The Index

Certainly each is placed in a volume for a specific reason. Which aids are included chiefly to aid the reader in locating information? An effective instructional program in subject matter should prepare a student to make efficient use of each part of a textbook for the purpose for which it was intended.

Of all the parts of a single volume that might contribute to the reader's location of information, the index is most efficient and profitable. The time taken to instruct a student in the efficient use of the index will be of continual value to him as he pursues the study of subject-matter material. The student must come to know the general arrangement of items in an index; he must understand the ways in which the reader is referred to specific pages; and he must understand the guide to cross-references. Without instruction in the use of an index, it is likely that a student will not use the index in an efficient way, and that his study of subject matter will suffer as a result.

Another important technique that needs to be employed in locating specific information in a single volume is learning how to attack the pages the student is referred to by the index. It is not likely that all the material to which the index refers is pertinent to the specific interest of the reader. Therefore, he should employ a technique that will enable him to locate efficiently that information which is most useful, and at this point his ability to quickly skim for information can be applied. A student, having learned that each sentence in a well-written paragraph makes a contribution to the topic treated in the paragraph, will read two or three sentences in the paragraph to determine if the topic of specific interest to him is being covered. If not, he should move on to the next paragraph, using the same technique. When coming upon a paragraph that does treat his topic of interest, he will delve deeply into its content. This technique, when employed judiciously, will enable the student to quickly and easily locate the information pertinent to his topic of interest.

Because in the early stages of studying subject-matter material single volumes are often put at the disposal of students, it is of great importance that the student learn early to locate material efficiently within a given volume. It is practical to consider special training to cope with differences in format among volumes as students attempt to locate information within any given piece of material. It is also essential for the subject-matter teacher to know just how independent a student is in his skill of locating information in a single volume. The amount of assistance or additional instruction to be given will be determined by this knowledge about each student in a class group. Suggestions for assessing each student's ability to locate information in a single volume have been provided in Chapter Three. Cooperative efforts of the faculty can bring about further independence on the part of each student to locate efficiently material within a piece of material.

## Library Skills Necessary for the Location of Subject-Matter Information

Many college students admit to a feeling of inadequacy in locating information in a well-equipped library, revealing that they had received little or no instruction in the efficient use of a library. Some weakness has probably been present in the earlier instructional reading program of these students. Many report that they were in college before they learned to use a library with even minimal efficiency. Thus many potentially fruitful years in school have failed to bring about an acquaintance with and an effective ability to use library facilities. The challenge today is to instruct children in using the library for enhancing their pursuit of subject-matter material as early as it is feasible to do so.

The card catalog is the key to the location of available material in the library. The teacher does not have to have a 'complete' library at his disposal to initiate the understanding and use of a card catalog. A simple, small file box containing cards (subject, title, and autbor) made out on a few books available in the classroom can be used to teach the basic skills necessary to using a card catalog. Such fundamental instruction will not confuse a student in his beginning stages of acquiring this skill.

Following the gaining of some rudimentary skill in using a card catalog, students could be taken to a library with a complete card catalog system and taught to locate the actual materials in the library. The student can learn how materials are arranged in the library and where various kinds of materials are located: books, special references, current periodicals, bound volumes of periodicals, research studies, pamphlets, and other materials housed in the particular library.

The student will soon realize that the card catalog does not lead him to all the most up-to-date material that might be available. One source in particular that the student should gain acquaintance with is the *Readers Guide*, both the regular unabridged and the abridged copies. He will learn how this resource can lead him efficiently to the most recent information on a subject-matter topic.

Special reference sections of a library should be pointed out to the student seeking subject-matter information. Encyclopedias, atlases, various who's who-type volumes, almanacs, and other special reference works can be of great assistance to him.

The pursuit of knowledge in a library can be a stimulating and profitable experience for a student who has mastered effective study techniques. If he has not, the experience can be frustrating, and the library may become a place to avoid whenever possible. The teacher of subject matter can readily meet the challenge of getting his students to feel at home in such a complex source of information by teaching skills necessary for effective study, and he can encourage a student's continual use of the facility through making meaningful subject-matter assignments.

### The Skill of Evaluating Printed Information

Success in locating what seems to be useful information is often so gratifying that a person may neglect the evaluation of that information before putting it to use. At times, this appears to be an almost unavoidable deficiency in study technique, even of otherwise mature persons. It is not uncommon to hear one person say to another, when asked whether certain information is valid, "I saw it on such and such a page of last night's newspaper." or "Mr. so-and-so just told me about it last night." The evaluation of information so freely accepted and disseminated is often sorely neglected; and this neglect is often initiated in the classroom where, of all places, it should be given thorough consideration.

As students progress through school, a tremendous amount of information is presented to them in printed form without adequate time spent in guiding them to evaluate the information. Think of your own school experience to date. What do you know about the hundreds of authors who wrote the books selected for your use as textbooks? Can you name the authors of even a dozen of the textbooks you've used? Do you recall your teachers spending time building for you some credibility for the authors of those textbooks in situations where it was not clear that the authors were well acquainted with the field about which they had written? If it was done, when did it begin—in the elementary school, the secondary school, or in college?

This portion of Chapter Two will be devoted to a discussion of the evaluation of information located by a student for possible use in a subject-matter course. Two main topics of evaluation will be discussed:

1. Is the information pertinent to the subject being considered?

2. Is the information valid?

The authors will also discuss the critical use of information, an act often neglected at any age level.

The importance of any information to a specific topic can only be determined by possessing a clear understanding of the problem (often in the form of an assignment) being pursued. When a teacher provides purposes for reading, as suggested in Chapter Five, such a clear understanding can be obtained. Much information is extremely interesting regardless of when it is brought to one's attention, but it is not always applicable to the problem at hand.

One writer recalls a situation reported to him by a sixth grade teacher. Students in his class had taken special assignments in which they were to research topics and report at a later date to the class as a whole. One student's report was on the Suez Canal. In presenting his report, he mentioned the very interesting topic of canal locks, describing the locks on the Suez Canal. At this point the teacher interrupted the report to inform the student and the class members that there were no locks on the Suez Canal. Locks were not necessary there as they are on many canals. (The teacher had taught a number of years in Africa and had an occasion to see and use the canal.) In his research on the Suez Canal, the student had neglected to apply a very important part of the evaluation process—determining the relationship of the information to the specific topic under consideration. The informed and alert teacher found a great opportunity to make this phase of evaluation clear to his students.

Assignment-making will be discussed at considerable length in Chapters Five and Six. But it can be made clear here just how important the assignment-making process is in teaching, as it provides the setting for application of an important phase of the evaluation process—determining whether information located is *pertinent* to the specific subject-matter topic. If a teacher assigns a purpose for reading which is clear, the student can quickly determine whether the information he has located is pertinent to the purpose.

The second major consideration in the evaluative process is that of establishing the validity of information located for possible use in pursuing subject-matter content. Teachers of young learners are usually held in high esteem by their students. Lack of experience brings out a certain amount of naiveté in all persons, but especially in the immature learner. He often takes as the gospel truth any utterance made by the teacher. The teacher, in turn, with a certain amount of naiveté, often conveys to the students the idea that whatever is found in print—chiefly the textbook—is probably true. A rather general attitude of acceptance of the idea that everything found in printed form is automatically to be taken as truth about the topic being considered seems to prevail. So often, this acceptance carries over into adult life—an undesirable situation, expecially in a democratic society.

A number of suggestions are presented here that, if taken seriously and practiced, might well promote the ability of students to more carefully and accurately validate information designed to be used in exploring subject-matter content. The purpose is not to develop excessive skepticism on the part of students as to the validity of information presented in printed form, but to initiate caution and the discipline of being willing to check out the validity of information.

Perhaps one of the first ideas about which to make students aware is that all material presented in print is not necessarily true. Material in print, expecially material used in a classroom setting, seems to be imbued with an aura of truth. Therefore, it is the task of the teacher to build as much credibility as possible for the material to be used by students in pursuing subject-matter topics. Textbooks, encyclopedias, atlases, reference books, periodicals, and newspapers,

## 28   Skills Necessary for Reading Subject-Matter Material

section by section, can be discussed as to the possible credibility that might be attached to them. It is here that authorship, copyright dates, publishers, and authors' sources of information should be brought to the attention of students.

From time to time in reading classes or in subject-matter classes, special lessons should be taught to point up how validation can be carried out by individual students as they consider the use of information found to be pertinent to the subject-matter topic at hand. The set-up for such lessons is treated in Chapter Six in some detail. Students should be taught to check on the qualifications an author possesses that make him prepared to write on the topic he has chosen. At certain levels of development the teacher may provide this information for students who will later employ the technique independently.

One of the writers of this textbook has often used this example in an attempt to make this point clear to students in pre-service teacher training classes. He asks them if, based on the knowledge they have of a prominent professor on campus, they would consider purchasing for use in their schools a science textbook series of which he is the senior author. Because of the size to which the university has grown and because only a few students even know who the professor is and the position he now holds, they are skeptical about considering the series for use. However, upon being informed concerning the academic honors and degrees the professor has earned, the previous positions he has held, and the fact that for years he has been the senior author of a science textbook series for the elementary school which is published by a prominent company, a measure of credibility is established for this professor. Yes, they would now consider the series for possible use.

Students should be taught to check statements made by an author at one place in his book or series with statements made about the same topic in another part of the book or series. Too, when doubt about a statement exists as found in one source, the student should be taught to check other sources. A comparison of two sources, for example, yielded a discrepancy of over 400 miles in the length of the Missouri River. Although this example may be relatively unimportant, it does point up the misconceptions that could be established due to failure to validate information.

A weakness that teachers often permit to enter the validation process is that of not particularly encouraging students to use their own experiences, limited as they might be, in validating information on a subject-matter topic. Teachers often neglect to seek accounts of personal experience from students that could help validate information reported in textbooks. Indeed, they too often discourage such contributions from students. It behooves a teacher to know his students well enough to be able to capitalize on experiences they've had for validating purposes. These may range from travel experiences to famous geographical or historical places, through experiences in extreme weather conditions—snowstorms, floods, tornadoes, to contacts with famous personages.

Besides these useful sources upon which validation of information can be based, a number of basic skills necessary for evaluation have been identified by several authors. The following skills can add to the student's ability to evaluate the worth of information:

1. Distinguishing fact from opinion
2. Identifying assumptions
3. Recognizing qualifiers (almost, some, perhaps, seemingly, usually, etc.)
4. Recognizing propaganda techniques

The list can be expanded considerably. What is more important to remember, however, is that the teaching of the ability to evaluate what is read should emphasize the development of an attitude. Hence, the teaching of evaluation can be impressional as well as skill-oriented. The teaching of skills alone, without the development of a concomitant attitude that what is read should not be accepted until it has been evaluated, will probably not develop mature readers of subject matter.

The necessity of teaching students the ability and the desire to evaluate cannot be overemphasized, because a person is constantly required to think critically as he faces situations in his lifetime. Few people escape the necessity. Although a given situation may not have developed from the individual's being brought into contact with printed materials, the answers may well have to be sought through the use of printed materials. It is at this point where the evaluation process is of greatest importance. The student in a subject-matter course who has developed an attitude of critical thinking will understand the need as well as have a mastery of skills in applying the techniques of evaluation that will result in his thinking, and subsequently, his acting critically in a situation demanding this of him.

## Organizing Information for Use

It is the assignment, as understood and accepted by the student, that should reveal the use to be made of information obtained through printed material. An ability to organize this information will assist greatly in its efficient and effective use. The organization of information is presented for discussion in this section of Chapter Two.

An assignment, well presented and understood, should also tend to suggest a suitable form the organization of the information will take. Although there are characteristics common to all forms of organization, specific situations will call for rather selected forms of organization. For example, if an assignment requires the rote memorization of information, the student's task of organization is minimal. If, however, an assignment is to prepare for an extended discussion or, perhaps, to make an oral report, the organizational task for the student will be quite different as well as more challenging. When an assignment calls for the student to memorize some printed information, he will likely attack the information, making little, if any, organizational change in the information as presented in the printed material. However, less structured assignments will require extensive use of organizational skills by the student. Let's consider some of these skills.

First, the student will need to take notes on the information he has found to be pertinent to and valid for the subject-matter topic. Succinct notes made on the information, preferably in the student's "own" words, will enable the student to organize these notes into a form most suitable for use in fulfilling the assignment.

The demands of the task of organization depend upon whether the collected information is obtained from one source or many. The nature of the assignment and the extent to which the student is permitted to use the notes taken for preparation of the assignment will also tend to dictate the form his organization of information will take.

Let's hypothesize that the assignment calls for the student to prepare an oral report to be presented to the total class at some future date. The only agreed-upon restriction, other than that of time, is that the report is not to be read orally from a prepared script. However, the student may use notes to aid him in making the report. The notes prepared for final use might well be made from a prepared, fully written paper.

The student must determine the form of notes that will best fit his needs. The one he might feel most secure with—a full script—is not available to him. Therefore, he has two other major forms to consider: (1) the summary paragraph or (2) the outline.

The summary paragraph is constructed from the script of the report, presenting only the major topic and sub-topics to be covered. Such an aid will contain little or no detail. Necessary detail will have to be recalled by the student making the report from the general information contained in the summary paragraph.

A summary paragraph is prepared in the following manner. The first sentence will be topical in nature, presenting the main thrust of the whole report. Each subsequent sentence will present, in brief, a sub-topic, placed in the paragraph in the order the student wishes to have it presented. A concluding statement might be placed at the end of the paragraph as an aid to the student in drawing the report to a close.

It can be seen that much of the substance and detail of the topic must be presented from what the student is able to recall "on the spot" while making the report. Considerable confidence is required on the part of the student to use the summary paragraph as his chief organizational aid in making the report.

Probably, for most students, the outline is the organizational form that will be found most useful as an aid in presenting an oral report. Considerable instructional time taken through the school years to help students develop the ability to outline information from which to present an oral report is justifiable. Although such instruction will no doubt be initiated in language arts subjects, primarily reading and English, it might be beneficial for the teacher of content subjects to remind students of the application of their ability to outline, thus assisting in continual development of the skill.

The title of the report itself may well be the title of the outline. Each major sub-topic will be placed in the outline so it can be readily observed as such by the student making the report. Many outline forms are in use today, each quite acceptable. However, the writers suggest that the school faculty and students adopt a suitable form to be used generally throughout the school. Such a practice will reduce the frustration that so often comes from needing to satisfy the outline form required by each individual teacher. A form such as the one below is one suitable form:

TITLE

I. First sub-topic
   A. Major detail
      1. Minor detail

II. Second sub-topic, etc.

The outline permits the person making an oral report to include as much detail as he feels is necessary. Most often items in an outline are not written in sentence form, but consist merely of a phrase, or even a word. The student has confidence that he can formulate the sentences he desires as suggested by the abbreviated form.

It is likely that the student making the oral report will be able to maintain much more eye contact with his audience when using the outline rather than a full script. The audience will likely be considerably more attentive to the content of the report when eye contact is continual. Too, the student making the report is in a better position to sense the attitude of the audience to the report and make adjustments to increase the report's effectiveness.

The content subjects often require the student to pull information from many sources. His ability to organize this information into a unified whole is essential to its eventual effective use. The teacher who checks on the extent of each student's ability to organize pertinent information and encourages the further development of each student to use such skills as he pursues assignments that require the use of printed materials is making a lasting contribution to the student's educational tools.

**Retaining Information for Use**

A study skill required of the student whose assignments ask for him to read printed material is that of retaining information for use. The use may be almost immediate or it may occur at some future time. The amount and kind of information to be retained will vary with the situation that prompted the specific assignment. Also, the assignment should, by nature, reveal the aids, if any, that a student may employ in retaining the necessary information.

An assignment may lead to an examination which, in some situations, demands almost total recall. Perhaps the assignment is to culminate in a discussion in which an individual's contribution will be drawn from information retained by him but not specifically assigned to him. Or, an assignment may be to prepare for making an oral report; in making the report the student may be permitted to use some aids to retention short of a script to be read. Two such aids—the summary paragraph and the outline—were discussed earlier in this chapter.

It is of primary importance for a student to realize that different situations demand various kinds and amounts of retention. Daily activities of the population in general require the retention of information, much of which is first gained through printed material. Although this is usually "spelled out" in a subject-matter course, a person must eventually acquire the ability to retain information in carrying out the common tasks of life.

Students are usually expected to read great quantities of printed material as they pursue a subject-matter course. For this reason alone, it is of practical use for the student to learn how to get the most from a single reading of printed material. There is just so much to read, and, unless something special and intentional is done by the reader, a single reading is not likely to contribute to much retention of information in proportion to the time used in reading it. Many techniques have been practiced with the hope that an amount of retention commensurate with the demands of an assignment will result. Underlining of what seems important to the reader is an example and a common practice among students, at least when reading personally owned material. It is questionable just how helpful such a practice is even though it is in common use.

A single reading can reap considerable benefits in retention of information if it is attacked with questions in mind that the reader expects the printed material to help answer. The kind of questions are dependent, again, on the nature of the assignment. Does the assignment call for selecting main ideas, providing detailed information, identifying the sequence of events, ascertaining a point of view, or one of a number of other specific kinds of information? The questions should lead the reader to 'zero in' on the information called for by the assignment. Multiple rereading of printed materials does not tend to aid retention of information if nothing of a special nature is done before the actual reading is carried on. A student will be gaining an important study skill technique if he is encouraged to employ the question-forming technique prior to the single reading of printed material called for in an assignment.

The writers, at this time, wish to call the attention of the reader to a technique for reading subject-matter material commonly called SQ3R. Although the terms are slightly changed the objectives of the technique are very similar. The employment of the technique should bring greater retention of information found in the material read, making it more useful for fulfilling a given assignment.

Let's dissect the formula bit by bit, stressing what each segment attempts to accomplish in promoting retention of information required by the assignment.

## SQ3R

1. The *S* stands for *Surveying*; the reader is to make an overview of the material to be read by noting a number of things that the material may contain, namely:
   a. Chapter title(s)
   b. Chapter section headings
   c. Specific quotes
   d. Italicized phrases
   e. Boldface printing
   f. Aids other than printed material that may by present—graphs, charts, diagrams, maps, tables, etc.

2. The *Q* stands for *Questioning*; keeping the assignment in mind, the reader now formulates questions that he believes the material to be read can help him asnwer. A concentrated effort is made to set up questions that are directly related to the assignment being pursued.

3. The first *R* stands for *Reading*; the student will now read the material, noting the parts of the material that appear to be most appropriate to the specific assignment. Some parts will be read initially with more care than other parts, for the reader realizes the material is more pertinent to his assignment. The rate of reading will vary as the difficulty varies and the need for the information the material contains varies.

4. The second *R* stands for *Reflection*; the learner is now encouraged to think about the information he has found as he relates it to the questions previously formulated. Through this process, the reader can sense areas that need more thorough treatment—perhaps, rereading.

5. The third *R* stands for *Rereading*; the reflection process will tend to point up the areas covered in the material read initially that need further treatment. This material may be reread with a concentrated effort to "dig" for the information it contains that is relevant to the specific assignment.

To just read printed material without a definite technique of attack is likely to result in wasted time. Continual employment of a technique similar to the SQ3R technique should tend to cut down this waste, making reading in the subject-matter area an act that promotes greater retention of information contained in the material.

# Skills Necessary for Reading Subject-Matter Material

## SUMMARY

The ability to read is not always employed by a learner in an efficient or effective manner. Any assignment (self-imposed or assigned by a teacher) should automatically call forth the application of very definite reading-study skills. In this chapter the skills of location, evaluation, organization, and retention have been discussed. Some authorities add other skills to this list and/or interpret the above in slightly different ways. The writers of this book believe that the successful employment of these four reading-study skills will do much to enable students to profitably study printed sources of subject-matter information.

## QUESTIONS

1. When an assignment requires the reading of subject-matter material rather than narrative material, why is the reader expectd to use additional skills?

2. List the skills a reader should use in fulfilling an assignment requiring the reading of subject-matter material. Why is each skill you've listed considered to be important?

3. Evaluate for possible personal use various procedures for retaining what you consider to be important subject matter met in your reading. Plan to discuss the merits of these procedures with other class members.

*CHAPTER THREE*

# Identifying Reading Strengths and Weaknesses of the Subject-Matter Student

There is no doubt that subject-matter concepts can be learned through media other than the printed page. A number of instructional techniques which do not include the use of printed material are presented in Chapter Seven. A skilled teacher can successfully employ these techniques to lead students to the successful study of subject matter. When printed material is not used, the reading ability of students is of little concern to the teacher. However, when printed material *is* used, the ability of students to read the material is of paramount concern to the teacher. When this is the case, a teacher who attempts to skillfully use textbooks and other printed materials will probably seek the answers to three questions concerning the reading ability of his students:

1. At which levels can each student read without help?
2. At which levels can each student read with help?
3. At which levels do materials tend to frustrate each student even though he might receive help?

A teacher might also want to determine whether the students who can read basic class materials independently or with help can use the materials as the authors intended them to be used. The teacher might then attempt to answer a fourth question:

4. Which students can use basic class materials efficiently?

In this chapter, three approaches to assessing the ability of students to read both basic and supplementary materials will be presented. Each approach provides information which can be used to answer one or more of the four questions identified above.

## The Informal Reading Inventory

Reading authorities have identified three levels at which individuals function in reading. These three levels—*the functional reading levels*—are identified and described in the following paragraphs:

**The Independent or Recreational Reading Level** is the highest level of reading at which the child can read fluently and with relative ease, and at which he can achieve good comprehension of what he is reading. At the independent reading level, the child can pronounce or say at least 98 percent of the words he reads, and he can correctly respond to 90 percent of the questions he might be asked about what he has read.

**The Instructional Reading Level** is the highest level at which a student can pronounce or say at least 95 percent of the words in a selection and accurately respond to 75 percent of the questions he might be asked about what he reads. At this level, the child shows no unusual signs of tension or frustration.

**The Frustration Level** is the lowest level at which a student begins to show signs that he is having difficulty reading the material. At this level, visible signs of tension or frustration often become obvious. The frustration level is often identified as the level which begins at the point at which the student does not pronounce or say correctly at least 95 percent of the words in a selection or at which he does not respond accurately to at least 75 percent of the questions he is asked. The upper limit of the frustration level is usually regarded as the point at which the student cannot pronounce or say correctly at least 90 percent of the words in a selection or respond correctly to at least 50 percent of the questions he might be asked about the selection.

A teacher who knows each student's functional reading levels can use this knowledge to good advantage. For example, suppose that in a ninth-grade history class a teacher has a student who has an independent reading level of sixth grade or lower. In assigning tasks which require independent reading—i.e., reading which the student will do on his own with no help from a fellow student, a student committee, or the teacher—the teacher can guide the student to materials written on a level at which the student can read fluently and with good comprehension. Such materials will not frustrate the student. They will not cause the student to dread independent reading assignments because he cannot succeed at them. It is likely that there will be fewer occurrences of incomplete or poorly completed assignments. Reluctance to participate in class or a dislike for the subject itself will also be less likely to take place if the student is guided to materials which he can read successfully on his own. Thus, a knowledge of each student's *independent* reading levels—the answer to the question, "At which levels can each student read without help?"—can be a valuable asset to a subject-matter teacher.

A knowledge of each student's *instructional* reading levels can also be a valuable asset to a subject-matter teacher. Suppose that the teacher knows that the instructional level of the student referred to above is the ninth grade level of difficulty. The teacher will then know that if he helps the student to overcome the problems posed by a given printed selection (see Chapter Five), that following the help provided by the teacher, the student will be able to read material ranging from seventh grade level through ninth grade level. (A technique for establishing the grade level of difficulty of materials is discussed in Chapter Four.) The teacher can be confident that, with help, the student can probably study his basic text(s) and other supplementary materials which are written at a ninth grade level or lower, even though the student can read independently without help at only the sixth grade level or lower. Establishing each student's instructional level answers the question, "At which levels can each student read with help?"

To enable a teacher to avoid assigning reading which will be too difficult for a student, even though the student might receive help from the teacher, a knowledge of the student's *frustration level* can be of value to the teacher. If the optimum instructional level of the student referred to in the preceding paragraphs is the ninth grade level, the student would probably have a frustration level which begins when he encounters material written at the tenth grade level. The student's tolerance for frustration might range from tenth grade level through twelfth grade level, depending upon the extent of his motivation or the content of the material. For example, a student might become frustrated, even though he has received help from the teacher, if he is required to read a selection entitled "Heat:

## FIGURE 3

*Constructing and Administering the Informal Reading Inventory*

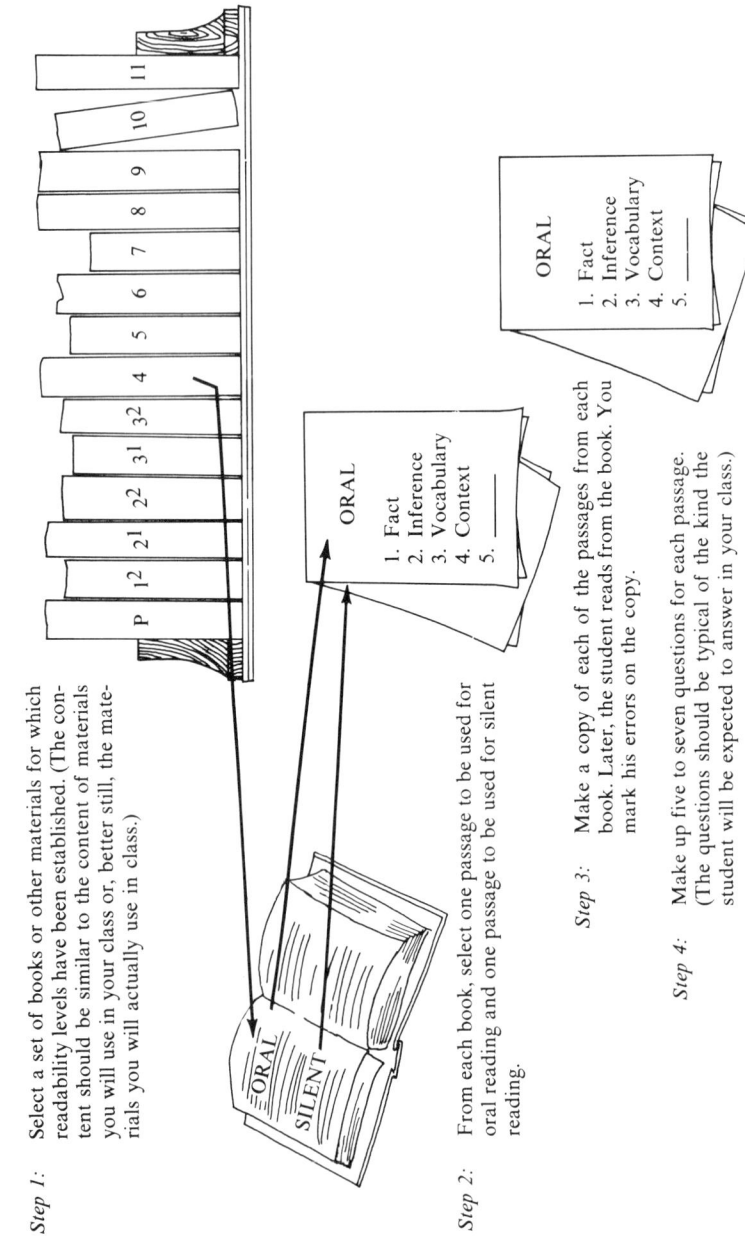

*Step 1:* Select a set of books or other materials for which readability levels have been established. (The content should be similar to the content of materials you will use in your class or, better still, the materials you will actually use in class.)

*Step 2:* From each book, select one passage to be used for oral reading and one passage to be used for silent reading.

*Step 3:* Make a copy of each of the passages from each book. Later, the student reads from the book. You mark his errors on the copy.

*Step 4:* Make up five to seven questions for each passage. (The questions should be typical of the kind the student will be expected to answer in your class.)

40

*Step 5:* Direct the student to read the first passage. orally. Mark and count his errors. Then ask him the questions which follow the oral reading. Count the number of questions he answered correctly. Direct the student to read the second passage silently. Then ask him the questions which follow the silent reading. Again, count the number of questions he answered correctly.

*Step 6:* Count the number of errors in oral reading. Subtract these from the total number of words in the first selection. This equals the student's raw score in word pronunciation. Add the number of correct answers to questions following the reading of the first selection to the number of correct answers to questions following the second selection. This equals the student's raw score in comprehension.

ORAL

1. Fact
2. Inference
3. Vocabulary
4. Context
5. _____

---

*The types of errors which are counted are presented in Appendix B. When the Informal Reading Inventory is used to diagnose specific skill deficiencies for purposes of *reading instruction*, careful attention is given to recording the *kinds* of errors a child makes. For establishing functional reading levels, however, the content teacher need only record the *number* of errors the child makes, since it is not the content teacher's responsibility to systematically teach word attack skills.

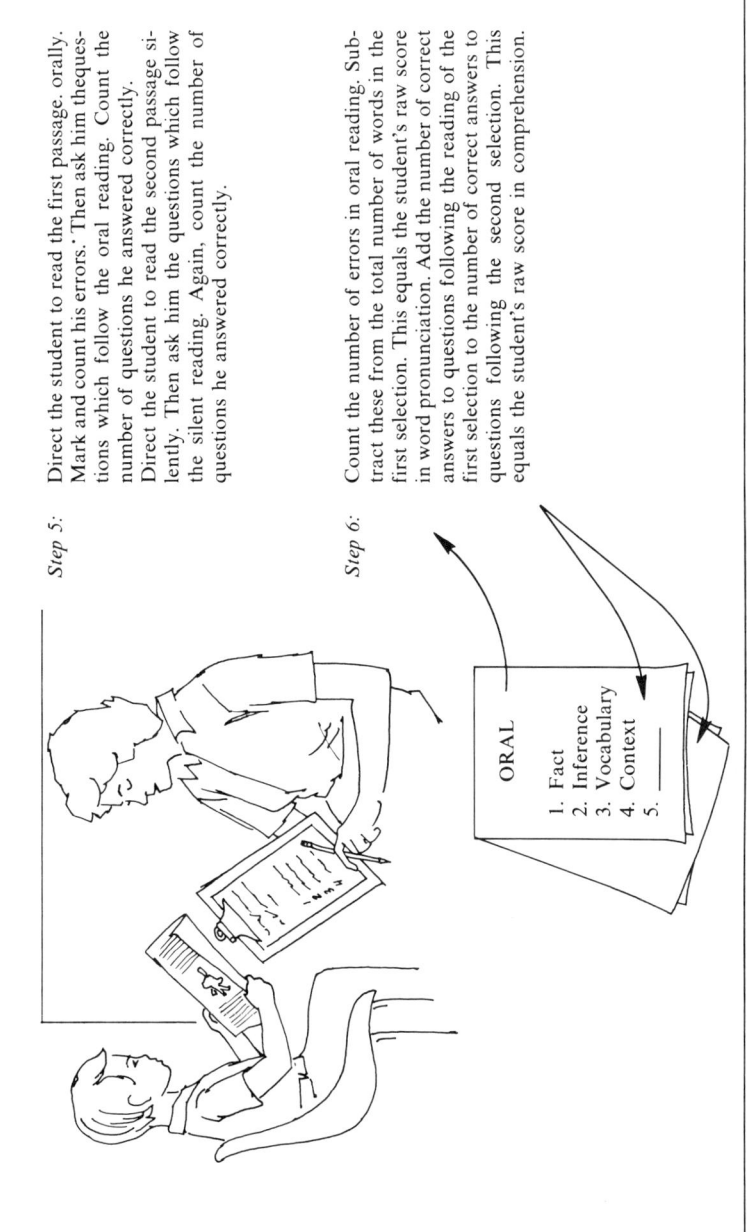

## FIGURE 3 (CONTINUED)

*Step 7: Determine percentages of accuracy.*

Oral Reading (Word Pronunciation)

$$\frac{\text{Number of Words Right}}{\text{Number of Words in Selection}} = \underline{\ 90\ } \quad \text{which} = \underline{\ 90\ } \%$$

*Example:*

$$\frac{180}{200} = 200 \overline{)180.00}^{\ .90} = 90\% \text{ accuracy}$$

$$\begin{array}{r} 180. \\ \hline 0\ 0 \\ 0 \\ \hline 00 \end{array}$$

---

Comprehension

$$\frac{\text{Number of Questions Right}}{\text{Number of Questions Asked}} = \underline{\quad}, \text{ which} = \underline{\quad} \text{ percent.}$$

*Example:*

$$\frac{13}{14} = 14 \overline{)13.0000}^{\ .957} = 96\% \text{ accuracy}$$

$$\begin{array}{r} 12.2 \\ \hline 80 \\ 70 \\ \hline 100 \\ 98 \\ \hline 20 \end{array}$$

Conduction, Convection, and Radiation," which is written at a tenth grade level of difficulty. If he has no strong motivation to read this material, he will probably fail to complete the assignment. On the other hand, if the student wants to pass the state driver's license exam, and if the state manual is written at a twelfth grade level,* the student will probably stick with the task of reading the manual if he receives sufficient help to understand the material, even though his "normal" frustration tolerance level for subject-matter materials might begin at the tenth grade level. The teacher who knows each student's frustration level, as well as his interests and needs, can help the student avoid reading experiences which are defeating to him. The teacher can also help him attain reading experiences which give him success. The answer to the question, "At which levels do materials tend to frustrate each student?" can be provided when a teacher establishes each student's frustration level.

### Determining the Functional Reading Levels

Each student's functional reading levels** can be ascertained through the use of an informal teacher-made test called the *Informal Reading Inventory*. Directions for constructing, administering, and scoring the Informal Reading Inventory for use in subject-matter classes have been presented in Figure 3 (see pages 40–42).

An example of how the functional reading levels for a student might be determined follows.

A teacher assumes that Keith, a student in an eighth grade science class, can probably read successfully on his own at a level of about sixth grade. To make sure Keith experiences some success on the Informal Reading Inventory, the teacher asks Keith to read first at the fifth grade level. Keith makes a score of 99 percent in word pronunciation and 97 percent in comprehension. The teacher then compares Keith's score to the criteria as shown in Table 1.

---

*Application of the Fry Readability formula indicates that driver manuals written at twelfth grade level or higher include the manuals of the states of Arizona, Wisconsin, Arkansas, and Ohio.

**The Listening Capacity Level, which is frequently used by teachers as a guide for selection of audio-visual materials and oral presentations, has been omitted from the discussion, since the focus of the chapter is directed toward enhancing student's *reading* success.

# Identifying Reading Strengths and Weaknesses

**TABLE 1**

|  | Criteria |  | Keith's Scores |  |
|---|---|---|---|---|
|  | W.P.* | Comp. | W.P. | Comp. |
| Independent | 98 | 90 | 99 | 97 |
| Instructional |  |  |  |  |
| Frustration |  |  |  |  |

*Word Pronounciation

Keith's scores are higher than the minimum percentages of accuracy established for the independent reading level. The teacher can assume that Keith's independent reading level is at least fifth grade level. However, it might be higher. Therefore, the teacher asks him to read at the sixth grade level (see Table 2).

At the sixth grade level Keith achieves 98 percent accuracy in word recognition and 92 percent in comprehension. Again, the teacher compares Keith's scores to the criteria.

**TABLE 2**

|  | Criteria |  | Keith's Scores |  |
|---|---|---|---|---|
|  | W. P. | Comp. | W. P. | Comp. |
| Independent | 98 | 90 | 98 | 92 |
| Instructional |  |  |  |  |
| Frustration |  |  |  |  |

Once again, Keith's word pronunciation score is not lower than the criterion. His comprehension score also meets the criterion. Now the teacher can assume that Keith's independent reading level is at least sixth-grade level.

The teacher now asks Keith to read material at the seventh grade level of difficulty. At this level Keith achieves 100 percent in word pronunciation and 88 percent in comprehension. Keith's scores, when compared to the criteria, look like Table 3.

Identifying Reading Strengths and Weaknesses 45

**TABLE 3**

|  | Criteria |  | Keith's Scores |  |
|---|---|---|---|---|
|  | W. P. | Comp. | W. P. | Comp. |
| Independent | 98 | 90 | 100 | 88 |
| Instructional |  |  |  |  |
| Frustration |  |  |  |  |

Since the score of 88 per cent in comprehension is lower than the minimum percentage of accuracy required at the independent level, the teacher can conclude that the *sixth-grade* level is Keith's independent reading level. At the seventh-grade level, it can be seen, Keith's scores did not meet *both* criteria associated with the independent level. Another look at Keith's scores, however, reveals the information in Table 4.

**TABLE 4**

|  | Criteria |  | Keith's Scores |  |
|---|---|---|---|---|
|  | W. P. | Comp. | W. P. | Comp. |
| Independent | 98 | 90 | (100) | 88 |
| Instructional | (95) | (75) |  |  |
| Frustration |  |  |  |  |

The teacher can see that Keith's scores are higher than the scores established as minimum percentages for the *instructional* reading level. Therefore, the teacher can assume that Keith's instructional reading level is at least seventh grade.

Next, the teacher asks Keith to read material at the eighth-grade level of difficulty. At this level, Keith achieves a score of 96 percent in word pronunciation and 77 percent in comprehension. Comparing Keith's scores with the criteria established for the instructional reading level, the teacher observes the information which appears in Table 5.

## 46  Identifying Reading Strengths and Weaknesses

**TABLE 5**

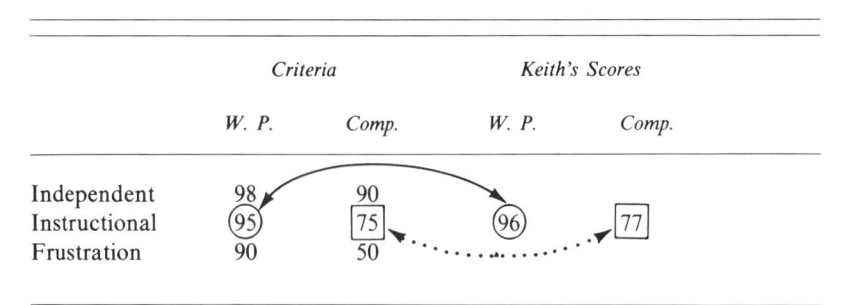

|  | Criteria | | Keith's Scores | |
|---|---|---|---|---|
|  | W. P. | Comp. | W. P. | Comp. |
| Independent | 98 | 90 |  |  |
| Instructional | 95 | 75 | 96 | 77 |
| Frustration | 90 | 50 |  |  |

Since Keith's scores are higher than the criteria at the instructional reading level, the teacher now knows that Keith's instructional reading level extends through the eighth grade.

The teacher now repeats the procedure he has followed, and asks Keith to read at the next higher level, the ninth grade level. At this level, Keith achieves 92 percent in word pronunciation and 80 percent in comprehension. A comparison of Keith's scores with the criteria at the instructional level is shown in Table 6.

**TABLE 6**

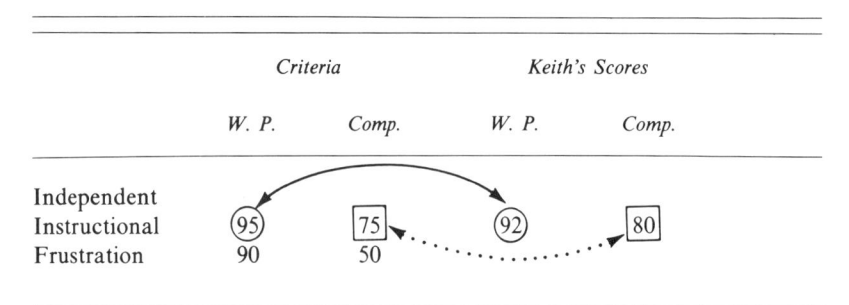

|  | Criteria | | Keith's Scores | |
|---|---|---|---|---|
|  | W. P. | Comp. | W. P. | Comp. |
| Independent |  |  |  |  |
| Instructional | 95 | 75 | 92 | 80 |
| Frustration | 90 | 50 |  |  |

Although Keith comprehended at a percentage higher than the percentage used as a criterion for comprehension, his achievement in word pronunciation was lower than the criterion in word pronunciation at the instructional level. Therefore, the teacher can assume that Keith's instructional reading level is *not* the ninth grade level. The teacher records Keith's instructional reading level as "eighth grade."

Another look at the comparison above reveals that Keith's word pronunciation achievement is above 90 percent, and his comprehension achievement is above 50 percent, the criteria for the frustration level. The

## Identifying Reading Strengths and Weaknesses 47

teacher knows that Keith's frustration level begins at ninth grade level. To find the upper limits of Keith's potential tolerance of frustration in reading, however, the teacher can ask him to read materials of increasing levels of difficulty, following the procedure in administering the test to this point, until he can no longer pronounce correctly at least 90 percent of the words he reads or comprehend at least 50 percent of what he reads. Then, the teacher can conclude that the upper limit of Keith's frustration tolerance is the highest grade level at which Keith pronounced correctly at least 90 percent of the words he read or answered correctly at least 50 percent of the questions following the selections.

After administering the Informal Reading Inventory, the teacher will have information about Keith which might be represented something like this:

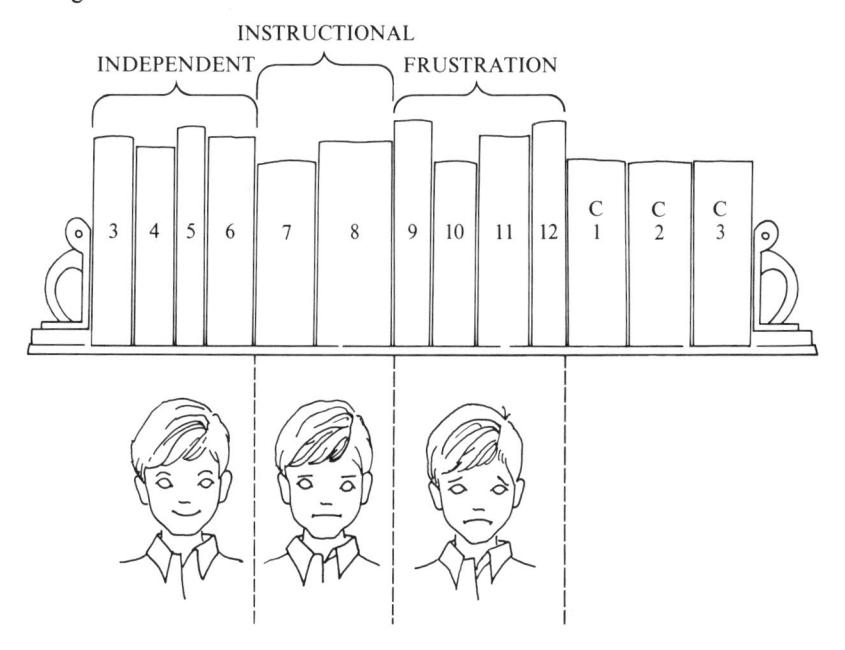

**FIGURE 4**

*Keith: Functional levels.*

The fact that the word "informal" appears in the name "The Informal Reading Inventory" is not accidental. The following considerations are worth keeping in mind when the Informal Reading Inventory is used in your classroom.

## Interpretation of Results

1. The results of an Informal Reading Inventory are an *estimate* of a student's abilities. The percentages used as criteria are important, but a teacher's observations of the student taking this test are equally important. For example, if a student achieves minimum percentages at any given level which indicate that he is achieving at the instructional level, and at the same time he behaves in a manner which indicates that he is extremely frustrated, use your professional judgement in establishing the level at which you think he can read for profit with instruction. Furthermore, if the results of the test differ dramatically from what your "teacher's intuition" and experience tell you, throw the test out and follow your own good judgement.

2. The grade level which is identified as a student's instructional reading level will be a valid estimate of the level at which he can read for instructional purposes *only* if he later receives instruction before reading selected materials at that level. If for any reason a teacher does not provide instruction to help a student read particular materials, or if the teacher's instruction is minimally effective, the student should not be assigned material at his instructional level. For example, suppose you are establishing a student's instructional level for another teacher who seldom provides more than a superficial introduction to a reading assignment. It would probably be wise to identify the student's instructional level at a grade lower than his true instructional level—the level at which he can read efficiently with *adequate* instruction. Basically, your placement can follow the idea that, with a good teacher, provide the true instructional level. With a less competent teacher, provide a level a little lower than the true level.

3. A factor to be considered in addition to the student's achievement on the Informal Reading Inventory is the student's ability to persevere: his "stick-to-itiveness." If you know that a particular student cannot stick to a reading task which requires diligent effort for more than a few minutes, make an appropriate adjustment in recording his functional reading levels. Referring again to Keith, if the teacher knows that Keith's instructional reading level extends from seventh grade level through eighth grade level, the teacher might record Keith's instructional level as "eighth grade." But if Keith cannot stick with lengthy reading assignments which require much effort on his part, it might be better to record his instructional reading level as "seventh grade." The demands on Keith will be reduced, and he may then be more likely to complete his reading assignments without needless difficulty.

## Quantity and Type of Material

1. Suggestions have been made in other sources regarding the length of selections to be used in an Informal Reading Inventory. However, since subject-matter material is more factual than it is narrative, and since ideas are presented in compact form and in rapid succession, prescriptions regarding the length of selections may be of limited applicability in making a subject-matter Informal Reading Inventory. It is suggested here that the length of a selection at any grade level be such that the selection is long enough to develop a basic concept and long enough to provide the teacher with enough material from which to derive questions typical of the kind he will ask in his class. Remember, though, that the longer the selections, the longer it takes to administer the test.

2. Graphic aids appear in abundance in subject-matter materials. This fact suggests that a question or questions at each level should be directed toward the interpretation or use of some aspect of any graphic aid which corresponds to a selection chosen for the Informal Reading Inventory. To ignore the student's ability to read graphic aids is to ignore a vital part of his subject-matter reading ability.

The Informal Reading Inventory is a useful instrument for a subject-matter teacher, but it can be very time-consuming to administer. Increased student ashievement resulting from placing appropriate materials in the hands of students suggests, though, that the time required for administering this test is time well spent. Nevertheless, the authors realize that time is of great importance to teachers, and that some teachers may desire an alternative method of assessment which can provide information similar to that provided by the Informal Reading Inventory. For this reason, the Cloze Test Procedure is also presented in this chapter.

## The Cloze Test Procedure

Another useful method which can be used in estimating the functional reading levels is the *Cloze Test Procedure.** The Cloze Test Procedure has been particularly attractive to subject-matter teachers who have

---

* Functional reading levels identified through the use of the Cloze Test have been found to approximate functional reading levels obtained through use of the IRI. (Duane S. Wiechelman, "A Comparison of Cloze Procedure Scores and Informal Reading Inventory Results. . ." Doctoral Dissertation, University of Northern Colorado, 1971).

## 50   Identifying Reading Strengths and Weaknesses

used it because it is an easy test to construct, administer, and score. It also provides an additional convenience in that it takes much less time to administer than the Informal Reading Inventory.

The Cloze Test, like the Informal Reading Inventory, is a test in which a student is asked to read selections of increasing levels of difficulty. However, the student's functional reading levels are assessed by determining the percentages of accuracy with which he can supply words which have been deleted from each selection. The percentages of accuracy achieved by a student are compared to percentages of accuracy which are the criteria for the functional reading levels on the Cloze Test.

Suggestions for constructing, administering, and scoring the Cloze Test follow:

*Step One:*   Select a set of materials which are either in use in your classroom or which are typical of those you would use in your classroom. From each of the materials, select a passage of about 520 words.

*Step Two:*   In each 520-word passage, delete every tenth word* until you have about fifty deletions. Replace the deleted words with blanks of uniform length. The only sentence from which words should not be deleted is the first sentence, which is left intact.

*Step Three:*   Ask the students to fill in each blank with the exact missing word which has been deleted. Do not provide the words in an accompanying list. Do not allow students to read the selection ahead of time. Each student should be allowed sufficient time to complete the test.

*Step Four:*   Count the number of correct responses provided by the student. A response is correct only if the exact word which was present in the original passage has been provided by the student. Do not count spelling mistakes as wrong answers, and do not count synonyms as right answers.

---

*The authors elsewhere recommend the deleting of every fifth word in narrative materials. [(Arnold Burron and Amos L. Claybaugh, *Basic Concepts in Reading Instruction: A Programmed Approach* (Columbus, Ohio: Charles E. Merrill Publishing Company, 1972)]. For subject-matter materials, it seems appropriate to follow Culhane's suggestion that an every-tenth-word count be used. [Joseph W. Culhane, "Cloze Procedures and Comprehension," *The Reading Teacher* 23,5 (February, 1970): 410-13.]

# Identifying Reading Strengths and Weaknesses

*Step Five:* Convert the number right into a percentage.

*Step Six:* Compare the percentage of accuracy on any given passage with the following criteria:

|  | Accuracy in Supplying Deleted Words in a Given Passage |
|---|---|
| Independent Reading Level | 57% |
| Instructional Reading Level | 44-57% |
| Frustration Level | Below 44% |

The procedure followed by a subject-matter teacher in administering the Cloze Test is similar to the procedure followed in administering the Informal Reading Inventory. If a student achieves a percentage of accuracy above the percentage of accuracy established as the criterion for any level, he is asked to complete a Cloze Test at the next higher level of difficulty. Suppose, for example, that Keith, the student who was tested with the Informal Reading Inventory, is also tested with a Cloze Test. His score at the fifth grade level is 53 percent. This score is above the minimum percentage of accuracy used as a criterion for the instructional reading level. He would then be asked to complete a Cloze Test based on a selection representative of the sixth grade level. Suppose his score is 47 percent at this level. This score is also above the minimum percentage of accuracy used as a criterion for the instructional reading level. Keith would then be asked to complete a Cloze Test based on a passage representative of the seventh grade level of difficulty, and so on, until his highest instructional level has been established.

## Other Uses of the Cloze Test

Although the Cloze Test can be used to provide a grade level designation for each of a student's functional reading levels, its real value to a subject-matter teacher is that of testing the "goodness of fit" of a particular book for a particular student. When a teacher wants to decide whether materials "fit" a student for instruction—that is, whether they are suitable materials for independent or teacher-assisted reading, the graded level of the materials can be ignored. The teacher then follows the procedure described below:

1. Select passages from materials you wish to use in your classroom.

## 52 Identifying Reading Strengths and Weaknesses

2. Construct Cloze Tests based on these passages.

3. Have students complete the Cloze Tests.

4. Compute percentages of accuracy attained by each student on each passage.

5. If a student makes a score of between 44 percent and 57 percent on any passage, you can probably assign instructional reading of the material from which the passage was taken. If the student achieves a score of 57 percent or better on any passage, you can probably use the material from which the passage was taken for independent or instructional reading. A score by a student of less than 44 percent accuracy on a passage would indicate that the material from which the passage was taken is probably not suitable for that particular student.

In using the Cloze Test as a test of whether materials "fit" the students you teach, you will not be primarily interested in estimating grade level designations for the students' functional reading levels. As long as you know which materials in use in your classroom "fit" which students, it is not essential to know grade level designations for the students' functional reading levels.

### Additional Considerations

1. The Cloze Test assesses, in part, the student's ability to infer from the context of a selection the words which have been deleted. Therefore, it is recommended that when the context does not logically imply particular words, the selection should not be used as material for a Cloze Test. For example, suppose a selection contains the following information:

> The menus of first-generation Manitobans of Eastern European origin would be strange to us. They regularly ate a variety of foods which included *oryshki* and other delightfully tasty deserts and pastries such as *strudel,* pephines, peppermint-flavored brenik, which was as hard as *pierogies* were soft, and revel küchen. For lunch, a sausage, *Kolbasa,* was served. In recent years, however, the children of *Ukranian* parents, like young people of German ancestry in this *area,* have lost much of the art of cooking these *exotic* foods.

The reader could not possibly infer from the context what words might have been deleted from this selection.

It is also suggested that the passages selected from subject-matter materials be those which present key concepts or key ideas, rather than those which provide easier to read *examples* of key ideas. The reason for this is that the purpose of administering the Cloze Test is to estimate the student's ability to read all of a selected piece of material. An accurate assessment would focus on his ability to read the most difficult parts of the material, rather than the easy parts of the material. Students who can read anecdotal illustrative material might not be able to read related paragraphs which contain the key ideas in a chapter.

2. The Cloze Test is an informal test. It provides, at best, an *approximation* of a student's ability to read selected materials. Hence, if the results of the test differ significantly from the teacher's carefully considered assessment of a student's ability, the teacher should feel free to disregard the results of the test until he has more opportunity to make a further assessment of the student. A teacher should not hesitate to be guided by his professional judgement and "teacher intuition" and disregard informal test results which differ significantly from his carefully considered judgement.

## Standardized Tests

The Informal Reading Inventory and the Cloze Test Procedure have been suggested as techniques which can be used in placing students into appropriate reading materials. The authors have deliberately avoided reference to standardized tests, with which subject-matter teachers are familiar, as vehicles for placement of students into reading materials. Research tends to support the contention that standardized test scores yield information which is not suitable for placement of students into appropriate materials.* Therefore, the authors recommend that scores derived from standardized tests not be used in matching students with materials.

---

* Research conclusions are similar to those reached by McCracken, who contended that the use of standardized test scores to determine the book level for instruction would place 93 percent of the students "in a book that is too hard for pupil and teacher comfort." (Robert A. McCracken, "Standardized Reading Tests and Informal Reading Inventories," *Education* LXXXII (Feb. 1962): 366-67.) Studies which have empirically demonstrated that standardized test scores are a most common indicator or a pupil's frustration level were enumerated by Farr, who recommended that "the use of standardized reading tests as indicators of instructional reading level should be abandoned." (Roger D. Farr, "Reading Tests and Teachers," paper presented at the IRA Convention, Boston, Massachusetts, April 24-27, 1968, p. 7.)

## Locational Tests

It was suggested at the beginning of this chapter that a subject-matter teacher would probably be able to teach more effectively if he could answer four questions about his students' ability to read:

1. At which levels can each student read without help?
2. At which levels can each student read with help?
3. At which levels do materials tend to frustrate each student even though he might receive help?
4. Which students can use basic class materials efficiently?

Answers to the first three questions can be obtained when the teacher uses either the Informal Reading Inventory or the Cloze Test Procedure. The importance of the teacher's obtaining an answer to the fourth question—"Which students can use basic class materials efficiently?"—has been suggested by Heilman, who states: "Students sometimes fail to realize that a number of reader-aids are included in most reference books and textbooks. Unfamiliarity with. . .these aids will inhibit students from mining books with maximum efficiency."*

The "in-book" locational skills which enable a student to use a book efficiently have been presented in Chapter Two. A sample of a part of a locational test—a test which assesses the students' ability to use "in-book" locational skills—follows:

SAMPLE QUESTIONS FROM A LOCATIONAL TEST**

1. On which pages of the book is Lord Selkirk mentioned? _____

---

*Arthur W. Heilman, *Principles and Practices of Teaching Reading*, 3rd ed. (Columbus, Ohio: Charles E. Merrill Publishing Company, 1972) pp. 490-91.

** Heilman (p. 490) suggests the use of a locational test as a testing *and* a teaching device. The test can be used effectively in this manner, and when the test is used for both testing *and* teaching, it is not necessary for the teacher to observe the third guideline in the discussion which follows. However, the authors recommend the use of a locational test for testing only, since it has been observed that a number of teachers regard their obligation to teach "in-book" locational skills as fulfilled upon administering an exercise of this type.

## Identifying Reading Strengths and Weaknesses 55

2. Which pages of the book provide the most information about Lord Selkirk? _____

3. Does the book include a picture of Lord Selkirk? _____

4. How did you find the answers to the questions above? _____

_____

5. The book includes a discussion of Metis. The part of the book which tells us about Metis does not directly tell us the meaning of the word. What is the meaning of the word Metis? _____

6. How did you find the answer to question five? _____

An examination of the sample questions from the test indicates that a student's ability to use the various parts of a book efficiently can be quickly determined. A few guidelines can be followed in order to make sure that the test readily provides you with the information you want.

Structure your questions so that the student cannot merely flip pages to get the answers. "Does the book contain a section which describes the westward movement?" would be an example of a question a student could flip pages to answer. If such a question is asked, it should be followed by a sub-question which asks, "On which page did you find the answer?" or "How did you find the answer?" An unsatisfactory response to these questions will indicate whether a student does, in fact, flip pages instead of using the appropriate book parts.

Sometimes the degree of mastery of a student's ability to use a particular part of a book can be assessed. The use of an index, for example, requires several levels of mastery of this skill. Some students know only that an index lists pages on which a particular item can be found. Others know that a reference such as "45-49" is probably of more use in finding information on a topic than a reference such as "38, 52, 112, 223." Still others know that a page reference in italics in an index might refer to a map or to an illustration. When several levels of mastery can be assessed, questions representative of each level of mastery should be included in the locational test. Several levels of mastery are suggested in questions 1-3 in the sample questions referred to on page 54.

As a teacher, your natural inclination when working with students is to teach them. Remember, though, that if you are trying to determine

## Identifying Reading Strengths and Weaknesses

students' ability, your test should not be a teaching worksheet. A question such as the one below, included in a locational test constructed by an experienced teacher who could not subdue her inclination to teach even while testing, is an example of a question for which the teacher has provided a partial answer.

> Look in the index for the heading 'Whaling.' Does this book include a map of areas in which whales are found?_____ Which letter behind a page number gave you this information?_____

Most students could probably easily answer the preceding question, but the teacher would not know which students have the ability to do this on their own in independent study.

Try to avoid questions for which more than one answer is correct. A question on the use of an index which can be answered if the student refers to a section entitled "List of Tables" will not provide a teacher with the information he wants concerning the student's ability to use an index.

Code the questions for yourself so that you can tell at a glance which questions refer to which book parts. Then, when you've obtained the results of the test, you can teach students the skills in which they are deficient. Requiring the use of these skills when you make reading assignments will reinforce your teaching of these skills. If the use of any skill is not required, it is probably a waste of time to teach the skill.

## SUMMARY

A teacher who seeks to use textbooks and other printed materials skillfully as vehicles for teaching subject matter will probably seek answers to four questions concerning the reading ability of his students:

1. At which levels can each student read with help?
2. At which levels can each student read without help?
3. At which levels do materials tend to frustrate each student even though he might receive help?
4. Which students can use basic class materials efficiently?

# Identifying Reading Strengths and Weaknesses

Three informal teacher-made tests—the Informal Reading Inventory, the Cloze Test Procedure, and a locational test—can be used in obtaining answers to these questions. The answers can be of value to a subject-matter teacher in assigning independent or teacher-assisted reading.

## QUESTIONS

1. Can the Informal Reading Inventory be used, as the Cloze Test Procedure is used, to assess the "goodness of fit" of a textbook or other printed material in appropriately matching materials with students, without reference to the graded level of difficulty of the material?

2. A common argument advanced by teachers of subject matter is that they do not have time to identify the reading strengths and weaknesses of their students. In discussions about the necessity of testing before teaching, the analogy of a tailor's taking measurements before making a garment has been used. Is the analogy appropriate in relation to subject-matter teaching? Assuming that no time is set aside for assessment, what consequences might ensue in a subject-matter class in which printed materials are an important part of concept development?

*CHAPTER FOUR*

# Evaluating the Textbook and Utilizing Reference Sources

After determining what the curricular content of a subject-matter course is to be, a teacher or a team of teachers can select resources to be used in teaching the course. The first step is often that of choosing a textbook that will fill the needs of treating the content to be covered. It is easier to choose a textbook for some subject-matter areas than others, for a number of conditions can determine the appropriateness of a textbook for a given group of students. The organization of the content, the readability level of its printed material, and the built-in aids (maps, charts, graphs, diagrams, tables, etc.) to assist concept development all need to be considered. Once a textbook is selected, continual adjustments in its use must be made considering the use of supplementary and complementary materials. It is the purpose of this chapter to help the reader to evaluate the textbook and to place it in its proper perspective, as well as to point out the tremendous advantages that can accrue from the effective use of reference materials as the objectives of a subject-matter topic are being fulfilled.

## Evaluating the Basic Textbook

The way in which a textbook is used is dependent upon the purpose for which it is used. A first step in evaluating a textbook either prior to or after selecting a basic text is to determine the major role the textbook will have for a particular course or unit. To guide the teacher in determining the major role of the textbook, the following checklist* can be of value:

Check and complete the major roles this textbook will have for a class and/or selected units.

____ Initial introduction to _____

____ Initial *printed* introduction to _____

____ Reinforcement of _____

____ Elaboration of _____

____ Supplement to _____

____ Alternative perspective for _____

____ Practice or application of _____

____ Enrichment activities for _____

____ Overview of _____

____ Specific detail for _____

____ Preparation for _____

____ Reference for _____

____ Review of _____

____ Fundamental content for _____

____ More challenging reading for _____

____ Easier reading for _____

---

* The checklist and several other suggestions have been adapted from "A Textbook Analysis Procedure" (developed for Badger High School, Lake Geneva, Wisconsin, 1972) by Robert Pavlik, University of Northern Colorado.

## Evaluating Textbook and Utilizing Sources 61

It is also helpful to evaluate other aspects of the textbook in order to make the most of the textbook as a teaching tool. The following items can be profitably utilized and expanded upon by a subject-matter teacher.

What types of graphic aids are present in the textbook? _____

_____

Which graphic aids will probably have to be taught to students? (pages) _____

For which graphic aids have students already mastered the interpretation skills? _____

Do transitional paragraphs explain the relationship of one chapter to previous related chapters, sections, or parts, or will it be necessary for me to provide a transition for the students? _____

Do concluding paragraphs or summaries adequately summarize main points, or is a teacher-assisted summary activity necessary following assigned reading? _____

Are opening paragraphs motivational? Does the content have appeal for my students? Will motivational introductory activities be necessary prior to assigning reading? _____

What potential barriers to understanding are posed by the material (see Chapter One)? _____

How valuable are the post-reading questions or application activities in relation to the purposes for which the book is intended? _____

_____

Do units in the book direct the student to readily available reference sources? _____

The major concept(s) developed by a particular unit is/are _____

_____

Ways in which I can further the development of this/these concept(s) without using printed material are _____

The evaluation of a basic textbook usually focuses on how a textbook will be used and on how suitable the textbook is for the purpose(s) for which it is intended. The items above are suggestions only; any teacher-made checklist or informal survey which attempts to answer questions regarding the purpose(s) for using a textbook and the suitability of a textbook in meeting these purposes can help the teacher successfully use the textbook as a teaching tool.

A significant factor often overlooked in the evaluation of basic textbooks is the readability level of the textbook. It seems logical to assume that the grade level indicated by the publisher of a particular text is an accurate indication of the readability of the text. Such is not always the case; studies of six different series in each of the areas of social studies, English, and science revealed that, in each subject-matter area, the discrepancy between the publisher's designation of the readability level of a text and the estimated readability level of the text using the Fry Readability Formula could be as great as three grade levels!* Usually the estimated grade level was higher than the level indicated by the publisher. In only a few instances were the publisher's designation and the estimated readability level in agreement. These findings seem to support Fry's assertion that "though readability formulas are used by... some publishers, their number is all too few."**

In view of the discrepancy between publishers' statements regarding the readability levels of their texts and the estimated readability levels of these texts, it seems desirable for a teacher to be able to independently assess the readability levels of his basic textbooks. Fry, in the article quoted above, presented a readability formula which can be easily and quickly applied by subject-matter teachers (see Figure 5).

A thorough evaluation of the basic textbook seems imperative if successful teaching with the textbook is to occur. The assessment of the readability of a textbook is an important part of the textbook evaluation process.

---

*Gail Barnes, "An Analysis of the Readability Levels of Basic Textbooks in Science, English, and Social Studies through the Application of the Fry Readability Formula," (Honors Project, University of Northern Colorado, 1973).

**Edward Fry, "A Readability Formula That Saves Time," *Journal of Reading* (April, 1968): 513–15, 575–77.

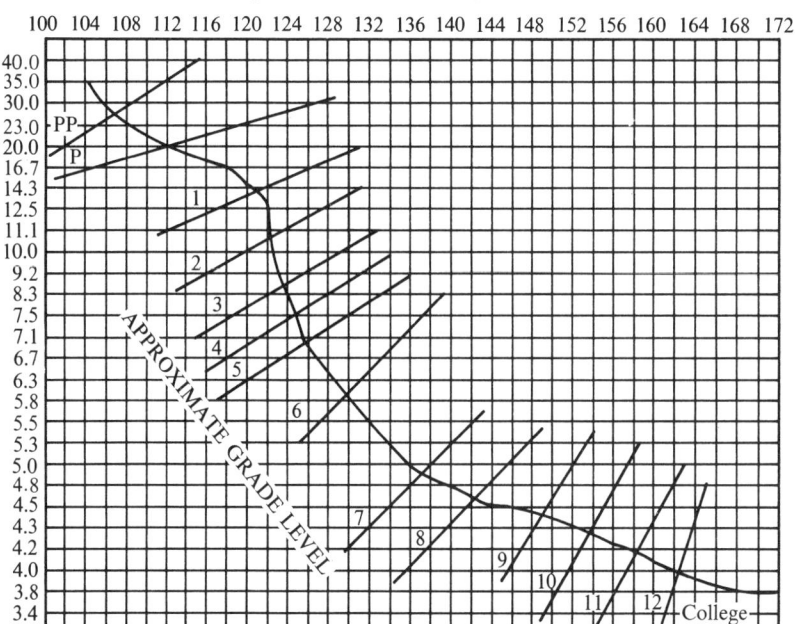

Evaluating Textbook and Utilizing Sources   63

[Graph: Fry's Readability Graph with "Average number of syllables per 100 words" on x-axis (100–172) and approximate grade level on y-axis (3.0–40.0), with grade markers PP, P, 1–12, College]

*Directions:* Randomly select three passages of one hundred words from a book or an article. Plot average number of syllables and average number of sentences per hundred words on graph to determine area of readability level. Choose more passages per book if great variability is observed. Skip all proper nouns.

**FIGURE 5**

*Fry's Readability Graph Extended Through Preprimer Level*

## Utilizing Reference Sources

It is not uncommon for students as well as the teacher to more or less assume that the selected textbook will carry the bulk of the load of instruction taking place in a subject-matter course. In fact, the content of a textbook is often the content of a subject-matter course both in scope and sequence. Such rigid adherence to a textbook in most content areas tends to minimize the effectiveness of treating a subject-matter topic.

Many restrictions are placed on an author as he attempts to treat subject matter in pages between the covers of a textbook. He may be told to limit his treatment to so many pages. A certain percentage of the total book must be given over to pictures and other less abstract material than the printed word. Size of print can be a limiting factor, too. Yet, the author is expected to concern himself with up to thousands of concepts within the textbook. At best, a textbook ends up being a limited treatment of content material using summary-type sentences but often lacking the detail necessary for adequate development of the content to be covered. The end result is not the fault of either the author or the publisher, for each has logical limits within which he must attempt the task of producing an adequate textbook.

Take what you consider to be a good textbook in some content area. Note closely its setup. It will no doubt set forth a scope and sequence of content that is logical and comprehensive. Yet, the author will indicate again and again in his book—from preface to index—the limitations of his treatment of the content in his textbook as published. The introduction will suggest his purpose, his proposed treatment, and the limitations of the content. The table of contents will outline the scope and sequence within which he is writing. Either at the end of each chapter or at the end of the body of the textbook, he is likely to supply an extended bibliography, suggesting that these sources will help support and amplify what he has been able to set forth in his book. In addition, a section of the book may give specific information or titles, authors, publishers, addresses, and costs of materials referred to in the textbook but which could not be treated in detail. Providing information on innumerable resources to be investigated beyond the textbook is a valuable contribution laboriously assembled by the author. Many years ago one of the writers of this short book was asked to assist a well-known textbook author in assembling a list of audio-visual materials that might complement the textbook material he was writing. The care the author used in selecting just those materials suited to his needs engendered additional respect for that author and the service he was attempting to provide the reader.

Some teachers find it inappropriate to begin instruction with the selected textbook but will initiate instruction at some less abstract level. Some teachers may use the textbook at the onset of a subject-matter course but only to set the scope and sequence of content to be considered. A teacher must know a textbook well to be able to sense its real value for a given student or group of students. The use of a textbook will vary according to the readiness of the students expected to use it, the objectives to be pursued, and the availability and utilization of complementary materials and activities designed to enhance learning.

Students will more likely use resources for learning beyond the textbook as the teacher instructs them in the location and use of these resources and as he exhibits the use of them himself. If a teacher implies that all answers are to be found in the textbook, students are not likely to seek information beyond the textbook. On the other hand, the teacher who is continually referring to sources of information beyond the textbook is likely to be getting across to students the value of these resources for comprehensive learning.

It is seldom that all resources alluded to by a textbook author are readily.available or could even be used thoroughly by students in a given subject-matter course, but through a selective process some can be used and will no doubt enrich the treatment of the topic being investigated. However, the student must be instructed in how to locate and use them. The advancement of the learner in the use of the reading study skills will determine the value he can obtain from resources beyond the textbook. For example, let's consider the resources of a library, basically text-type materials—other textbooks, books treating specific topics in quite thorough detail, periodicals that treat the topic, monographs, and even research studies relative to the topic. Encyclopedias, almanacs, atlases, pamphlets, etc. also have great possibilities for enhancing the topic under consideration. Can the learner at his stage of development seek out these materials independently or must he be led to them until further instruction in locating them is provided? The teacher must know at what stage each student is in his ability to employ location skills, be it in the use of a card catalog that leads him to the library stacks where what he is seeking is located, in using the *Readers Guide* that will enable the student to locate efficiently material to be found in periodicals, or in locating information in a single volume or smaller source by using the table of contents or the index provided.

The stage of development possessed by each learner will determine the extent that a teacher can expect independent use of these resources by the student. If the resource material is deemed important to the content being considered, the teacher may have to assist the student until independence is reached. Much instructional time is wasted when students fumble through resources in an inefficient way as they seek material that could prove very helpful in concept development.

All schools have not determined just where the responsibility lies in preparing students to successfully locate information beyond the textbook pertinent to a topic. It is generally conceded that the major task of the content teacher is to bring important subject matter before the student. But for a subject-matter teacher to be ignorant and unconcerned about the extent a student is able to locate and use sources beyond the textbook is inconceivable. This he must know about a student, and he must do something about it, in conjunction with other teachers—the reading teacher, the librarian, or other subject-matter teachers. Cooperation in this task is essential to the progress of the learner in utilizing valuable resources for learning beyond the textbook.

It takes months, often years, to get a textbook published. Although the bulk of the material is basically sound, students could be "shortchanged" if more current resource materials were not considered in teaching a content area. Weekly and monthly magazines, daily newspapers, recorded speeches, and radio and television presentations should be considered as possible valid and up-to-date sources of information. A teacher should be prepared to adjust to new and revised data coming forth since the publishing date of the selected textbook. The teacher must be "on his toes" to capitalize on whatever resources are made available that can update the subject-matter topic being pursued. Recent experiences of the teacher and/or the students might well prove to be an acceptable resource to the topic at hand.

A separate chapter in this book (Chapter Seven) will treat the utilization of so-called audio-visual aids in teaching content subject matter. These resources can be valuable additions to the sometimes limited treatment of topics by textbooks. One of the writers recalls his teaching of the traditional fifth grade unit "Westward Movement." Specifically he recalls the importance placed upon the hardships faced by the pioneers in meeting their needs for obtaining food, clothing, and shelter for the family. A great deal of importance was placed on the part the long rifle played in the life of the pioneers as a tool for obtaining food and for maintaining protection for the family. However, in looking through a number of textbooks, the writer could find little or no detailed reference to this important tool, the long rifle. By chance his attention was drawn to some books other than a textbook. In this case, it was one of Laura Wilder's books entitled *Little House in the Big Woods*.* In this book he found, written at a third-grade level, a complete chapter just on the long rifle. The

---

*Laura Wilder Ingalls, *Little House in the Big Woods* (New York: Harper and Row, 1932), Chapter 3.

detail provided seemed to support the importance that was alluded to in the selected textbook. Other chapters in this particular book covered in detail major activities faced by pioneers who were part of the Westward Movement. A teacher needs to be aware of sources of this nature that can enhance concept development, whether it is in social studies, science, mathematics, or any other subject-matter course. Occasionally first-hand accounts of pertinent experiences that can truly enhance the topic under consideration are reported in current publications.

Reenactments of past events are authentic only to the extent that research has been complete enough to enable the cast to portray what actually took place. Credibility can be established for a production, as a whole or in part, and this can be pointed out to the students using it for learning. Aids to learning are available that can help overcome the obvious shortcomings of a textbook. The extent to which these are incorporated in instruction, with their limitations made obvious, will be resources that can enhance the learning of any subject-matter course. It is primarily tha task of the teacher to seek out these resources, make them available to his students, and promote the proper utilization of them in subject-matter courses.

## SUMMARY

A thorough evaluation of the basic textbooks to be used in a subject-matter class will consider elements of the textbook related to three main questions:

1. What is the purpose for which the textbook will be used?
2. How suitable is the textbook in relation to the purposes for which it will be used?
3. What is the estimated readability level of the textbook?

A sample informal checklist and the Fry Readability Formula were suggested in this chapter as avenues through which answers to the preceding questions might be approached.

Limitations of textbooks and advantages in using reference materials were also presented. It was suggested that the limitations of textbooks can be compensated for through the judicious use of reference materials by students who require instruction in the use of these reference sources.

## QUESTIONS

1. The Fry Readability Graph is a useful tool in assessing the approximate readability level of a selection; nevertheless, the graph can be misleading. Which characteristics of expository writing does the Fry Graph not take into account (see Chapter One for related information)?
2. Why is it important to consider the use to which a book will be put as well as the readability level of the book?

*CHAPTER FIVE*

# Capitalizing on Knowledge of Students and Materials

In Chapter Three, three methods of assessing the reading strenths and limitations of students were suggested, and Chapter Four presented ways of evaluating textbooks. In this chapter, suggestions on how to use the information thus obtained about students and materials will be considered. Two questions will be answered:

1. How can I individualize instruction?
2. How can I make meaningful reading assignments?

## How to Individualize Subject-Matter Instruction

Many teachers who have taken the time and invested the energy to assess their students' functional reading levels have expressed amazement upon discovering the wide range of reading ability among their students. One of the authors remembers his own amazement and consternation when, in his beginning years of teaching, he discovered that instructional reading levels in his sixth grade classroom ranged from first grade level through tenth grade level. If you, the reader, are an experienced teacher, you are well aware of the fact that the usual feeling which follows the discovery of such a wide range of achievement is the feeling of panic. This feeling is usually followed by a decision to "individualize" instruction. Few teachers, however, believe that they can initiate and sustain an "individualized" program, principally because their concept of individualized instruction is that of one-to-one teaching. They believe that a teacher must teach children one at a time if individualization of instruction is to occur. This idea is erroneous; it has probably defeated more teachers who made a conscientious effort to provide for individual differences than it has helped, because the task of providing one-to-one teaching is so monumental and impractical that most teachers cannot or will not attempt it.

There are two steps toward successfully meeting the challenge of the wide range of reading achievement which exists in your classroom. The first step is to recognize that there are degrees of individualization of instruction. Individualization can take place without one-to-one teaching. The second step is to accept the idea that you can find a degree of individualization which fits you, your students, and your unique teaching situation.

Three classroom variables can be manipulated by you to achieve varying degrees of individualization of instruction. For purposes of discussion, these variables are called "teacher input," "materials," and "student output." A brief description of each variable follows:

*Teacher input:* Any method used by a teacher to convey information, develop ideas, or encourage thinking prior to assigning independent study. Teacher input includes lectures, demonstrations, discussions, and the use of audio-visual materials or equipment, all of which will be discussed under "Presentation of Content" in Chapter Six.

*Materials:* Any source to which the student can turn in order to expand upon the information, idea, or concept introduced through the teacher's input. The student might independently listen to a tape, watch a film, read a chapter, conduct research, or utilize any other resources which might be available.

*Student Output:* Any project, assignment, or other activity which is required by the teacher as practice or as evidence of the student's understanding of the information, idea, or concept developed through teacher input and materials used.

When no manipulation of variables takes place, no individualization of instruction takes place. For example, consider a classroom in which no individualization of instruction is occurring. There are thirty students. The teacher provides one presentation in the form of a filmstrip which introduces a concept in science. There is no attempt to adjust teacher input to groups of students. Each student has the basic text for the class, and all students read the same chapter. There is no attempt to match students with appropriate materials. After reading the material, all students reproduce a diagram and answer three questions prepared by the teacher. There is no attempt to provide assignments which match student's abilities or interests. Furthermore, the teacher expects the same level of achievement from each student.

Now consider a classroom where a degree of individualization is taking place. The teacher, like the first teacher, provides only one presentation in the form of a filmstrip which introduces a concept in science. Each student reads the same chapter. After reading the chapter, however, some students are assigned the drawing of a diagram and the completing of questions prepared by the teacher. Other students are directed to additional reading. Still other students are required to observe some slides. The only variable which was manipulated was the variable of student output; nevertheless, some individualization of instruction took place.

Another classroom might provide evidence of the manipulation of two variables. In this classroom, the teacher, like the other teachers, provides one presentation in the form of a filmstrip. The teacher then asks students to read about the presentation in one of several books which are available. Students are then provided with one of several assignments. In this classroom, an even greater degree of individualization has taken place.

Manipulation of variables and the corresponding degree of individualization is shown in the diagram on page 72. The right hand side of the diagram shows no manipulation of variables, and, hence, no individualization of instruction. The left hand side of the chart shows manipulation of all three variables, and, hence, a great degree of individualization of instruction. The middle parts of the chart show manipulation of one or more variables and the corresponding degree of individualization of instruction which can be accomplished.

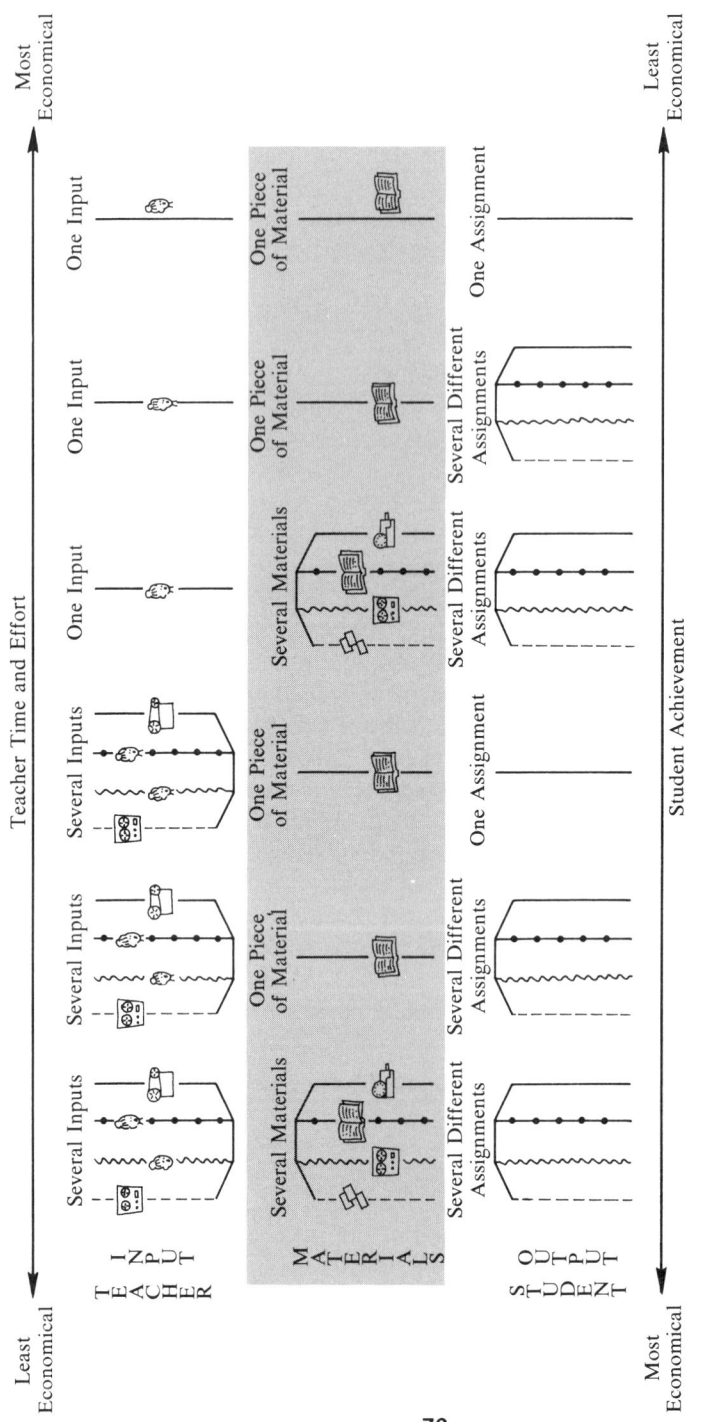

**FIGURE 6**

*Degrees of Individualization*

A look at the diagram reveals that when a teacher spends no time and expends no effort in attempting to individualize instruction (top arrow, right side) students will probably have to spend much time and expend much effort and attain only very limited results (bottom arrow, right side). What is economical for the teacher is not economical for the student. Conversely, as the teacher spends more time and effort in attempting to individualize instruction (top arrow, left side), the student will probably need to spend less time and expend less effort in attaining greater gains (bottom arrow, left side) than he achieved when his time and effort were not properly directed. When this occurs, what is increasingly less economical for the teacher is increasingly more economical for the student. Simply stated, the less time and effort a teacher puts into manipulating variables to meet individual differences, the more time and effort a student will have to put in, and the student's time and effort will probably be unproductive. The more time and effort a teacher puts into manipulating variables, the less time and effort a student will have to put in, and the student's time and effort will probably be more productive.

The main idea illustrated by the diagram is this: *Individualization of instruction occurs in varying degrees.* Somewhere along the continuum shown in the diagram there should be a plan which fits you and your teaching situation. You should feel free to tackle individualization of instruction only at the level which you can comfortably handle. As you gain expertise and confidence in manipulating variables, you can increase the degree of individualization you are able to attain. The important fact to be confident about is that you will be individualizing instruction the moment that you take a beginning step toward manipulating one of the three variables.

## Manipulating Variables Effectively

Your knowledge of your students' functional reading levels and your knowledge of the readability levels of your materials can be put to good use as you begin to manipulate variables. If any variable requires the student to read, you can match the student with appropriate materials. For example, if you provide instruction related to a reading assignment before making the assignment, you can provide material written at the student's instructional reading level. If you want the student to read independently without your prior teaching of the material, the material he reads should be that which is written at a level of readability which corresponds to his independent reading level. (Information provided in Chapter Four offers suggestions for estimating the grade level—the readability—at which a piece of material is written.)

If one decision you make concerning reading assignments is that you will provide instruction related to the assignment before asking the student to read, besides the general suggestions on assignment-making presented in Chapter Six, several specific steps can be followed in order to make the reading assignment meaningful. These steps are considered below.

## Making Meaningful Reading Assignments

A student's reading of an assignment at his instructional level can be highly productive if the teacher assists him in overcoming reading problems posed by subject-matter materials. Such assistance can be provided in the form of five steps taken by the teacher before asking the student to read.

FIVE STEPS TO MEANINGFUL ASSIGNMENTS*

Step 1. *Induce Interest* in the Assignment.

Step 2. *Build Background* for Understanding.

Step 3. *Provide a Preview* of the Material.

Step 4. *Suggest Purposes* for Reading.

Step 5. *Provide Related Reference Materials.*

### Step One: Induce Interest in the Assignment

In Chapter One, it was pointed out that a major factor contributing to student difficulties in reading subject matter is the problem of a low level of student interest in much subject-matter material. Therefore, a logical first step to follow in making meaningful reading assignments is to induce interest in the topic if it seems likely that students will have a low level of interest in reading about it.

---

* Arnold Burron and Adolph Christenson, "Reading in the Content Fields" (In-Service booklet, Spokane, Washington Public Schools, 1971).

### Knowledge of Students and Materials 75

The author recalls a situation in which a teacher anticipated that students might have very little interest in reading a selection about exploration in a sixth grade social studies text. The teacher decided to try to induce interest in the topic even before the students saw the first page of the proposed reading assignment. The teacher began by asking "experience" questions, questions related to students' personal lives. The lesson proceeded along these lines:

Teacher: "How many of you have someone in your family who watched the football game on television last Sunday afternoon?" (At this point, almost every student in the class raised his hand.)

Teacher: "I can tell that some of you also watched the game, along with some member of your family. I didn't get a chance to watch. Who was playing?"

Danny: "Minnesota and Green Bay. Minnesota won."

Teacher: "When those two teams play, it's usually a knock-down-drag-out battle. They usually have close games."

Bruce: "Well, that's what happened. Except for the Viking's runback on the kickoff, it was a tough game. Maybe the weather was too cold. The announcer said it was below freezing. They were wearing tennis shoes, and. . ."

Teacher: "Just a minute, Bruce. Something you said made me wonder about something. Bruce said the Vikings had a runback on the kickoff. How many of you know which team the Vikings are? Minnesota or Green Bay?" (A loud groan and derisive laughter from the boys followed this question. No doubt the teacher's question struck them as incontrovertible evidence of their teacher's supreme ignorance.)

Teacher: (Laughing) "Okay, okay, I know you know. But how many of you know how the Vikings got their name?"

Karen: "I know how the Packers got their name."

Teacher: "How was that, Karen?"

Karen: "I think it had something to do with a packing house in Green Bay."

Brian: "Ya. I remember that."

Teacher: "I think the Packers received money from a packing house in Green Bay; I think you're right, Karen. But what about the Vikings? Any ideas?" (After a brief pause broken only by a few muttered wisecracks about possible sources of the team name, it was apparent that an answer was not forthcoming.) The teacher then proceeded: "Well, I think they probably took the name from history. There's a story which is believed by many people in Minnesota (here the teacher pointed to a map) that Minnesota was visited by explorers before Columbus discovered America. The story probably got started when a farmer by the name of Olaf Ohmann had an unusual experience.

"In 1898, Olaf Ohmann was plowing a field in Minnesota when his plow hit a large stone. Mr. Ohmann started to move the stone when he suddenly noticed some strange writing carved in the stone. He became very excited and shared the news of his discovery with everybody he saw, but nobody could figure out what the writing said. Finally, after some length of time, somebody—I think it was a professor from the University of Minnesota—figured the writing out. The writing said that in the year 1362, one hundred and thirty years before Columbus, Swedish and Norwegian Vikings had explored Minnesota. The writing also told several other things about the Vikings which I won't go into right now, but if you'd like to find out more, I think the whole story can be found under 'Kensington Rune Stone' or 'Vikings' in the encyclopedia. Anyway, I think the Minnesota Vikings' name must be related to a farmer's discovery in a field way back in 1898."

Susan: "Do all team names come from history?"

Larry: "No. Couldn't be. What about the Colts?"

Teacher: "I think you have a good point there. But in some cases, even though the team name isn't based on something in history, the city name is. I think you'd be surprised to find out how many teams have names based on history, like the '49ers, the Canadiens, the Padres—or geography, like the Twins—and how many cities have names based on history. Let's take a look in our book at the section entitled 'Exploration.' I'm going to be asking you to read parts of this section, and I think that after you read certain parts, you'll learn quite a bit about how many major league teams in all sports and many major league cities acquired the names they now have."

The brief discussion described above took only a few minutes, but it served to induce interest in the topic. The students in the class seemed eager to read. The teacher had not succeeded in inducing interest on the part of all students—such an achievement is rare—but by following Step One in making meaningful subject-matter reading assignments, the teacher was able to help students overcome one major barrier to effective content reading.

## Step Two: Build Background for Understanding

In Chapter One, a lack of an adequate background for understanding was identified as a factor contributing to students' difficulties in reading subject matter. Teachers can provide numerous examples of misconceptions by both children and adults because an adequate background in a subject was lacking. Before deciding upon what background to build, a teacher need only to ask, "What prior knowledge does the selection assume the student has? Does the student have this knowledge?" In reading this chapter, for example, you can build upon your understanding of the term "functional reading levels." The authors assumed that, as you read the part of this chapter which dealt with the independent and instructional levels, you had a prior knowledge of the meanings of these terms. Many selections assume prior knowledge on the part of students.

If a selection assumes prior knowledge on the part of students, the next question a teacher might ask is, "What can I do to bridge the gap between the student's background of experience and the concepts presented in the material?" At times, background knowledge is readily built. For example, suppose a teacher wants to develop several lessons on the theme of "courage" in a literature unit and that one of the incidents chosen to illustrate courage is the story "David and Goliath." Full appreciation of the story is unlikely if the students are aware only of the fact that David, a boy, defeated Goliath, a large man. A mere explanation of the fact that Goliath was a superb Phillistine warrior over ten feet tall, accompanied by an indication of how high ten feet really is, say by referring to the height of a basketball hoop, would take less than a minute, but the explanation would add substantially to children's full appreciation of David's courage.

At other times, it may take a teacher considerably longer to build background, but if a child fails to fully understand or appreciate what he is reading because he lacks background, omitting the background-building step could negate much of the teacher's hard work in the preparation and teaching of a lesson.

## Step Three: Provide A Preview of the Material

It would be hard to find a subject-matter teacher who does not introduce new vocabulary in a selection before asking students to read the selection. In fact, the introducing of new vocabulary is sometimes overdone. Sometimes the introduction of vocabulary is detrimental to students' growth in the use of study skills. A teacher can be selective about introducing new vocabulary, since new or seemingly difficult vocabulary can be classified into three categories:

1. Words which are in the reader's listening and speaking vocabulary: The reader can probably figure these words out on his own through using the context in which the new words are found.
2. Words which are not in the reader's listening and speaking vocabulary but which are defined in a glossary or dictionary in a manner such that their intended meaning in the selection is clear.
3. Words which are not in the reader's listening and speaking vocabulary and which might contain an affix or be defined in a manner which would tend to confuse the student regarding their intended meaning in the selection.

The first two types of "new" vocabulary can be left for the student to conquer. The third type is appropriately introduced to the student by the teacher. A teacher who introduces every new or difficult-looking word to his students denies his students the opportunity of applying subject-matter reading skills in a meaningful situation. Application of reading skills can be fostered, though, if the teacher quickly groups "new" or "difficult" vocabulary according to the categories above.

Other steps in providing a preview of material are also desirable if obstacles to reading subject matter are to be overcome. The teacher can do the following things:

1. Point out difficult portions of the assignment and preteach concepts presented if it seems necessary to do so.
2. Suggest to students which parts might be skimmed, and why they can be skimmed.
3. Discuss graphic aids and their role in clarifying the material.
4. Point out typographical clues.
5. Call attention to figurative language, to the necessity to interrupt one's reading to refer to other book parts, or to any unusual aspects of style or format.

6. Identify the major concept developed by selection. Try to develop the major concept by explanation, examples, charts, pictures, graphs, models, the actual item, films, resource people, or other sources.

The preview provided by a teacher will not only help the student to overcome barriers to comprehension in subject-matter reading; the preview will also serve as a model for the student in conducting his own preview as he pursues independent study. Conducting a preview or survey is an important and effective study technique.

## Step Four: Establish Goals for Reading

It was stated at the beginning of this chapter that a teacher can individualize instruction by manipulating the variable of student output. Student output is individualized when the teacher assigns for a given selection reading goals which are consistent with a student's abilities. A few different kinds of goals or purposes for reading are listed below:

### GOALS FOR READING

1. Reading to answer a specific question posed by the teacher or the student
2. Reading to identify details in a selection
3. Reading to ascertain the theme, main idea, or major concept
4. Reading to verify or refute a statement or argument
5. Reading to collect all information relative to a specific question
6. Reading to obtain directions
7. Reading to discover the sequence of events

Many other goals or purposes for reading can be identified by a teacher. A goal or goals which provide a minimal challenge to a student might be appropriate for a struggling student. Suppose a teacher wants a fifth grade student to read about the early days of Texas in a social studies text. The teacher might say, "Alan, I'd like you to read to find out the reasons why early settlers went to Texas, what problems they faced in settling Texas, and how they overcame their problems." For a more advanced student, the teacher might assign a goal such as, "Read this selection about early days in Texas. As you probably guessed when we looked

## 80   Knowledge of Students and Materials

at the picture on page 181 (the teacher provided a preview of the material) there was a disagreement between the Texans and Santa Anna. Try to compare the problems of the Texans and the problems of the Mexicans. Then tell what the two sides might have done to solve their problems without fighting." Both statements by the teacher reflected the first two goals in the list above. However, the teacher made one question more difficult than the other in order to provide for individual differences.

Goals can be individualized and stated orally, or they can be written and selected students directed to read for selected goals on the written list. Goals can be stated as questions and students can be directed not only to read for answers but to be ready to support their answers by indicating which portion of the selection provided clues for attaining answers to specific questions.

The practice of a teacher's establishing goals for reading can help the developing and immature reader in forming the attitude that reading should be conducted with a purpose in mind. When this attitude has been acquired, the student will have developed one important ability which is characteristic of the mature reader and the serious student—that of reading for a specific purpose.

### Step Five: Identify Appropriate Reference Materials

The chapter on problems posed by subject-matter materials identified the problem of "compactness" as a detriment to effective reading of content material. Obviously, it is to be expected that any text which purports to be comprehensive must be selective and succinct in presenting what other sources have isolated as the most outstanding ideas germane to a given topic. Titles such as "A Survey of American History," "Exploring the New World," or "Science for Today" must necessarily exclude some important ideas, lest the basic texts assume the dimensions of an unabridged dictionary. In addition, basic textbooks and materials are written for the "average" child in the "typical" grade. If effective teaching of subject matter is the teacher's primary goal, a large measure of assurance of reaching this goal can be provided if the teacher compensates for the cursory treatment of topics in basic texts. This can be done when students are provided with material which they can read, and which provides supporting information which parallels the basic text.

This means, then, that an abundant variety of material which covers the topic selected for emphasis must be made available, including easy-to-read textbooks from lower grades and advanced reference materials suitable for serious research. One history teacher, for example, regularly

## Knowledge of Students and Materials 81

attends rummage and garage sales in quest of old history textbooks which discuss topics covered in his basic text. He conducts a quick readability check on the books, color-codes them according to their readability by using colored tape, and then attempts to match the appropriate student with the appropriate book. Books on his reference shelf are often used in place of the basic text, which might be inappropriate for certain students. His shelf includes the following titles and copyright dates, which often fascinate and motivate his students. The cost of each used book is also shown.

Faris, John T. "Real Stories from Our History." Boston: Ginn & Co., 1916. $ .25.

Gordy, Wilbur F. "A History of the United States for Schools." New York: Charles Scribner's Sons, 1898. $ .35.

Hart, Albert. "School History of the United States." New York: American Book Co., 1918. $ .10.

Kelty, Mary G. "The Beginnings of the American People and Nation." Boston: Ginn & Co., 1930. Free.

──────. "The Growth of the American People and Nation." Boston: Ginn & Co., 1931. $ .10

──────. "The Story of Life in America." Boston: Ginn & Co., 1941. $ .15.

Moon, Glenn W. "Story of Our Land and People." New York: Holt, Rinehart, & Winston, Inc., 1944. $ .25.

Tryton, Rolla, and Lingley, Charles. "The American People and Nation." 1927. $ .10.

Vannest, Charles, and Smith, Henry. "Socialized History of the United States." New York: American Book Co., 1918. $ .10.

An industrial arts teacher in the same school also has many supplementary materials available for students, most of which were obtained at minimal or no cost from private industry and federal and state agencies.*

To a determined teacher, there is little validity to the plea, "But we don't have the money for a variety of reference materials." A

───────────

* Several references from which sources of free and inexpensive materials can be obtained are listed in Appendix C.

variety of materials to supplement or to substitute for the basic text should be a "must" for subject-matter teachers who are interested, not necessarily in teaching reading, but in more effectively teaching subject-matter.

## SUMMARY

This chapter was directed toward providing suggestions for responding to two questions subject-matter teachers are called upon to answer.

1. How can I individualize instruction?
2. How can I make meaningful reading assignments?

It was also suggested that the first step to take toward successfully meeting the problem of the wide range of reading achievement which exists in a class is to recognize that there are degrees of individualization of instruction. It was then suggested that the extent to which a teacher can successfully manipulate one or more of the variables of teacher input, materials, and student output will determine the degree of individualization he can attain.

Five steps to follow in making reading assignments were recommended as a procedure to follow in striving for meaningful reading assignments. These steps were:

1. Induce Interest in the Assignment
2. Build Background for Understanding
3. Provide a Preview of the Material
4. Suggest Purposes for Reading
5. Provide Related Reference Materials

Adopting a degree of individualization which is both comfortable for and convenient to the teacher, and making reading assignments which are meaningful can lead to sustained student growth in subject matter achievement. Increased student ability in the reading of subject matter is a concomitant benefit.

## QUESTIONS

1. Select a chapter from a subject-matter text. Assume that you are manipulating the variables of "materials" and "student output." Identify several different sources to which students could be directed which could serve as a substitute for the basic text. Describe several different assignments which students might be given which would be related to the chapter you chose.

2. For the chapter you selected above, or for another chapter, describe the preview you would provide for students before asking them to read the chapter.

3. Provide several different purposes for which students might read the chapter you selected above. Try to provide purposes which would be appropriate for both slow readers and more accomplished readers.

*CHAPTER SIX*

# Using Instructional Time Effectively

Regardless of the number of instructional periods that have been allotted to the teaching of a subject-matter course or a unit within a course, conscientious teachers attempt to use each period to the best advantage of the learner. Nevertheless, it is not uncommon to find precious instructional minutes whiled away in the pursuit of activities which are not readily justifiable and which add little, if anything, to the development of the learner. In this chapter suggestions regarding the advantageous use of the instructional period will be considered.

All suggestions discussed in this chapter need not necessarily occur in each instructional period, yet each can be applied in the ongoing process of instruction. Major topics discussed herein are factors to consider in the following:

1. Assignment-making
2. Guided Study
3. Presentation of Content
4. Stimulating Discussion
5. Evaluation and Measurement of Learning

## 86 Using Instructional Time Effectively

Also to be set forth in this chapter is a set of criteria to be applied in planning for the presentation of a lesson—whether the lesson deals primarily with a concept to be understood, a skill to be mastered, or an attitude to be engendered. The criteria will suggest the conditions and the restrictions to be employed in any lesson of instruction in order for a lesson to meet a learner's needs.

## Assignment-Making

The making of an assignment is such an important activity that it deserves a more prominent proportion of instructional time than it commonly receives in most classrooms. So often assignment-making appears to be a "spur of the moment" activity that leaves little time for clarification. It is not uncommon for assignments to be given after the bell has sounded ending the class period. Probably more common is the placement of a "pages-to-be-read" assignment written on a chalkboard near the exit of the classroom where it is expected all students will be certain to see and comprehend it at a glance.

An assignment, to be realistic and effective, must incorporate close communication between the student and the instructor. Each must sense the topic to be explored, its relative importance, and the sources and/or procedures through which it can be explored. It is the responsibility of the instructor to motivate the learner to a point of desiring to explore the topic and helping set purposes, understandable by the student, for carrying out the assignment.

When a student leaves a classroom with an assignment, he should be in a position to pursue the assignment independently, needing assistance from no one. If such is not the case, the assignment is probably unsuited to the learner. How many times in the past has the reader felt the necessity to confer with someone else about some phase of an assignment? Why do telephone calls increase among learners in the early evenings, the time when at least some students have set aside, voluntarily or involuntarily, a time for doing their homework? The writer is reminded of a group of college graduate students who, upon finding it virtually impossible to conclude just what the professor expected of them regarding assignments, met after each class period to decide just what *was* intended and prepared to present a united front at the next class session.

To be right for a learner, an assignment must incorporate many factors, each of which should be based upon the knowledge the instructor has of the student. One such factor is the background the student has upon which to build what the assignment is designed to develop. A second factor is related to available resources that are compatible with the ability of the student. Here we are concerned with reading achievement of the learner and the readability level of the material to be read in pursuing the assignment. Out-of-class homework so often has been in material that a learner could not handle effectively even when in the presence of the instructor. A third factor to be considered is the time factor. Is the assignment controlled so that the time required to accomplish it is reasonable in view of assignments the student is likely to receive from other subject-matter instructors?

In order to give proper attention to the above factors, time from instructional periods must be provided. At times assignment-making may be a time-consuming activity, especially when the assignment will require effort on the part of the student over an extended period. At other times assignment-making may be a short-time activity, requiring the setting of a short-term objective that can be accomplished in a relatively short period of time, yet suitable for the learner. Attention to the preceding factors can be provided by a teacher through following several specific steps to making meaningful assignments. These steps, discussed under the heading "Five Steps to Meaningful Assignments" have been presented in Chapter Five.

## Guided Study

It is justifiable to use portions of instructional periods for guided-study activities. Here students carry on projects relative to subject-matter topics under the guidance of the instructor. The instructor is available at all times to assist in the efforts of his students. Stemming from well-established assignments at any given point in a learner's education, he is capable of carrying on activities with only a measure of independence in an effective and efficient manner. The instructor must know each learner well enough to realize when the learner can be encouraged to carry on an activity independently and when it is appropriate to give assistance to the learner. The subject-matter instructor appears, at times, to be utterly unaware of the extent to which his students are capable of carrying on a task, a task that requires, for example, locating information, extensive outlining, or preparing a report. Although it is not the primary responsibility of the subject-matter instructor to initiate these skills, it is desirable and helpful to him to know to what extent each student has progressed in his ability to apply these skills in carrying on assigned activities.

Although an assignment may seem very appropriate as far as concept development is concerned, the manner in which it is to be pursued may not be. Perhaps the following examples will help make this point clear to the reader:

1. Early in the first grade year, a science instructor directed the children to bring notebooks and pencils to class (a special science classroom was provided in the school) for the purpose of taking notes.

2. A third grade child who had received no prior instruction in locating information was asked to locate ten references in the library dealing with a specific subject-matter topic.

3. A sixth grade child was assigned to make a twenty-minute illustrated oral report to the other twenty-nine class members on a specific subject-matter topic.

In each example above, the instructor would no doubt have to give considerable assistance to the learner, for, at each of these grade levels, it is not likely that the student would be advanced enough in the application of the required skills to apply them effectively and efficiently. An assignment that requires the advanced application of a skill should be accomplished by teacher guidance so that the end product of the assignment can be obtained.

One writer recalls a specific situation that occurred in a fifth grade classroom. It was ten minutes before dismissal time. The teacher reminded the students that each had been working on a special report for some time and, if someone was ready to present his report, ten minutes was now available for a report or two. Two or three hands went up, and one student was called to give his report. As the student moved to the front of the room, he was pulling a folded sheet of paper from his rear pocket; the paper had been folded about four times. As he stood before the class, the student attempted to read something that he was obviously unprepared to do, for it was evident that he had merely copied some encyclopedia statements at some previous time and had done nothing further with them. As an observer in the room, the writer noticed immediately the embarrassed look on the instructor's face, who surely was instantly aware of his failure to have given guidance to the student in preparing his report. A great deal of precious instructional time is lost in just such situations, not only for the child carrying on the activity but also to the other students, who had a right to expect to gain valuable information from the report.

The teacher of subject-matter content, although his chief responsibility is seen to be that of developing concepts and skills laid out in the curriculum, must be continually aware of each student's ability to pursue the exploration of these concepts and skills independently. In addition, the teacher must not only be available to the learner but he should exhibit a willingness to assist the learner in ways that will enable him to complete his current assignment without excessive difficulty.

It seems pertinent at this point to stress the practical value of having the school faculty agree upon an acceptable uniform pattern for students in a school to follow in such practices as outline form, placement of identification on papers, and medium to use in writing. So much unproductive time can be spent by learners as they try to adjust, sometimes period to period, to individual whims or requirements of specific instructors when an agreement among faculty could avoid this.

## Presentation of Content

The teacher of subject-matter content has never been in a better position from which to choose the most appropriate means for presenting content information to his students. In fact, the problem facing the instructor is more one of choice than of a lack of suitable materials, equipment, and facilities.

To discuss the presentation of subject-matter information, let's envision a situation in which needed information must be brought before the learners. The instructor has a number of choices of input media. His immediate problem is to decide which medium or combination of media is most suitable for his particular situation. Although a more detailed discussion as to how materials to be read can be effectively complemented by other instructional aids appears in a later chapter, it seems appropriate at this juncture to discuss a variety of presentation techniques.

The writer recalls a visit he made to the classroom of the school's science teacher. The visit had been prearranged. Either by coincidence or deliberate planning on the part of the science teacher, each class group (one of grade four, one of grade five, and one of grade six) was being

## 90  Using Instructional Time Effectively

introduced to a new unit in science. This was done by asking the students to read the first one or two paragraphs of a given chapter to find what the new unit was to be about.

The environment in which these introductions were made was extremely sterile. The teacher sat at his desk; the children sat at their desks, which were arranged formally. Although an acid-resistant demonstration table was in the room, it was not brought into use. None of the materials or equipment in the adjacent storeroom were being utilized. The bulletin boards and chalkboards were devoid of material. The only apparent source of information being made available to the learners was the textbook.

A major question to be considered here is: Were there more appropriate ways by which this science teacher might have introduced these units to the students? Additional questions which might be asked to guide a teacher in presenting content include the following:

1. Is each learner ready to enter the topic through the medium of the printed page?

2. Is the printed page the most appropriate medium through which to motivate the learner to want to pursue the topic?

3. Would a less abstract medium than the printed page be a more appropriate medium through which to enter the topic from the standpoint of initial understanding?

4. Is the teacher in a position to use his own knowledge and experience in an effective way as a substitute for a textbook introduction?

5. Are the individual differences that surely exist among learners being met by a teacher in using only a textbook to introduce a topic?

It is well to consider questions of the nature of those above when the purpose of the use of a time period is to present information to the learners.

It is also helpful in conveying information if it is clear to the learners as well as to the teacher just what learning objective faces the group in a specific class period. The teacher, knowing the learners well enough to realize the base each has for concept development, can attempt to select a mode of presentation that will be most likely to bring about the desired learning. Because of the inevitable differences among learners, the teacher can usually use a combination of modes to ensure maximal growth in learning with all students in a given group.

It is at this point in a teacher's planning that he surveys the resources available to him in an attempt to find what he believes will best ensure the desired learning. At the onset, it is likely that only rarely will it be the textbook or other printed matter that achieves this end. More concrete avenues for learning are likely to be employed. Will it be a carefully planned field trip? Will it be a demonstration previously organized and rehearsed? Will a sound motion picture film or filmstrip be best for this particular group? Can the chalkboard, one of the earliest audio-visual aids, be put to use in a dramatic or dynamic way? Will maps and globes used in combination be the best things to use to begin concept development? Would a carefully planned lecture by the teacher accomplish just what seems to be needed at this time by this particular group of learners? Or is the material provided in the textbook today's answer to the presentation problem facing the particular group on a specific day?

Presentation time in a content area is usually so precious that it is essential that it not be wasted on ineffective procedures. When both the teacher and the learners are aware of the learning task facing them and when the mode(s) of presentation are appropriate for the task at hand, the probability that the desired learning will take place is increased. The teacher has a two-fold job:

1. He must know the subject area so well that he can map out a sequence of learning experiences designed to bring about the desired learning.

2. He must know at just what stage each learner is so that the most appropriate avenues of learning can be taken to increase the likelihood that the desired learning takes place.

## Stimulating Discussions

The portion of an instructional period set aside for discussion is usually viewed by teachers as an important time period. It is helpful, though, if the learner also understands its purpose—to stimulate the flow of ideas for broadening concepts, for clarification of mistaken ideas, and for encouraging both personal involvement in problem-solving and further learning. Such understanding dispels the idea on the part of the student that discussion is a special time period when he will be judged, and perhaps even "pigeonholed," because of what he says or asks as a discussion proceeds. Rather, the learner will be able to sense a freedom to explore ideas that supposedly have emanated from serious preparation for just such a period.

It is not at all uncommon for a discussion period to be grossly misused. In the past, and, at time even currently, learners are assembled only to be asked questions by the teacher as if an oral quiz were taking place. Too, the questions asked are often very factual in nature—not conducive to initiating a stimulating discussion. At times teachers use the discussion period to have students reread aloud materials assigned earlier to be read for an upcoming discussion. In some cases the teacher reads the material aloud for the group, knowing that the majority of the learners in the group will not have been successful in their "homework," a situation which occurs when assignments are indefinite and/or the materials used for preparation are at the frustration level for the learner. This happens frequently in content subject areas.

For example, one writer remembers a situation in a "discussion" class which occurred many years ago. The class was a 1:00 P.M. high school English class where the diagramming of sentences was the topic. Admittedly unprepared to diagram every sentence in a list, he desperately tried to save face by concentrating on those sentences most likely to be allotted to him as the oft-repeated routine pattern of questioning employed by the teacher inexorably advanced through the classroom. Damp palms can be recalled; the feeling of threat hung in the air. The only desire for freedom at that moment was not a desire for freedom to learn; it was the desire for the freedom of escape.

The writer also recalls visiting a social studies classroom at a time when a new class group was being assembled. The teacher was heard to say, in substance, that he knew the particular assignment had probably not been read so he might as well read it aloud for the group. All that seemed to be accomplished in the period was that a previous assignment was read by the teacher who, from time to time, asked some shallow, literal level questions about what he had read.

An effective discussion cannot take place in a pool of ignorance. Each discussant can be assisted by the teacher in preparing himself to make a knowledgeable contribution to the topic at hand. Providing each student with a purpose for reading relative to a subsequent discussion is one method of assisting students in making a meaningful contribution to a discussion.

In initiating a discussion, "experience" questions seem to be particularly helpful in eliciting a response. Experience questions are questions which allow the reader to draw from his personal background those situations which are analogous to the topic under discussion. For example, a discussion of serendipity in research could begin with a question which asks students about an accidental beneficial discovery they might have made in their own lives. In asking experience questions, it is obvious that the teacher takes an active part in the discussion. Thereafter, the teacher may moderate the discussion and interject pertinent questions and ideas along with others, but he attempts to refrain from dominating the talking or stemming the flow of ideas. As a discussion period draws to a close, the teacher can again assume an active role by summarizing salient points and by setting the scene for a future discussion. The desired result is that each learner in the group will feel that he has gained from the experience and can pursue further the topic because of interest, need, or new knowledge attained through the discussion period.

## Evaluation and Measurement

There are appropriate times for the evaluation and measurement of learning progress within the instructional period. It is when a teacher is asked, "Are you primarily a teacher or a tester?" that he may be shocked into realizing that testing, in one form or another, may be taking up the bulk of the instructional period.

Too often, the major portion of most instructional periods is taken up by some form of testing techniques—from paper-pencil tests, through graded worksheets, to out-and-out question-answer sessions, all of which tend to put the learner on the defensive. New or additional learning may be thwarted when such is a continual occurrence.

True, an alert and observant teacher is continually evaluating the ongoing learning scene. His knowledge of the day-to-day growth of his students is gained through many informal and non-threatening avenues of observation; e.g., Mary comes up with more weighty questions than she did in the past. Bill is bringing into daily discussions ideas not wholly confined to the adopted textbook. Arlene seems much more independent in her search for materials in the library. Bob is finding direct application of the skills introduced recently in the mathematics class. Susan sticks to her reading assignments for a much longer time than she used to. Alice is beginning to express herself in more conventional communication skills; English is certainly becoming a useful second language for her.

Map symbols are beginning to give Bob far less trouble than previously; he even keeps the directions straight when referring to a map. Jim seeks the help of others only occasionally now as he explores new books he wishes to read.

Such observations can be made in any number of situations, in circumstances completely devoid of student awareness that evaluation is going on. This is as it should be.

Measurement, however, is a different matter. When it is taking place, both the teacher and the student should realize it. People generally want to be aware of progress taking place and are quite willing to accept a process that will reveal it. Thus, tests or examinations ought to be administered periodically. Bench marks set at one time serve as points of reference to observe the progress that has been made.

The setting for tests is recognized as being different from those in which other activities take place in an instructional period. The learner knows the time has come to reveal his knowledge and/or skills relative to a rather specific area. Being slightly "keyed up" is not uncommon. A well-informed and adjusted individual should be able to weather the situation, realizing that both strengths and weaknesses are likely to show up.

The teaching-learning environment can promote the idea and practice that the purpose of most testing is for the improvement of instruction, either with or without the direct guidance of the teacher. Time is rarely wasted when tests are discussed after administration and scoring is complete. It is likely that better rapport between student and teacher, as well as improved learning, will result from such practice.

The writer recalls a course he was once taking in photography. The course required many and varied projects as well as tests. The occasion recalled was a test on which the writer felt he had done quite well. Surprised at the score he received, especially on one section of the test, he mustered the courage to discuss it with his professor. The end result was two satisfied persons—the student and the professor! Neither had to cajole the other, and each learned from the situation.

## The Presentation of a Lesson

Suppose that it has been determined that a higher step in a sequence of learning is essential to an individual or a student group. The instructor is faced with the task of initiating advancement in a skill or the acquisition of new or additional, but related knowledge in a content subject area. What conditions are essential for instruction at this point to be effective?

First of all, it is important for the instructor *to identify* what is expected to be gained from the instructional experience. To do this, he must know the level of knowledge or skill possessed by each member of the group receiving instruction. The next step, then, will seem logical to the student. It is likely that the student will say to himself, "I do need to know this or be able to do this if I'm going to move on, or up, or improve. Let's get at it."

The writer, like so many persons, admittedly prefers to practice what he can do in a present real situation rather than use time to initiate a new technique that would likely bring about improvement in his performance in a later real situation. Today, the area is golf; when in grade school and high school it was basketball. Today he forestalls taking that lesson or lessons that might result in bringing his score down a point or two. Years ago it was a slight resentment for having to practice free throws, pivoting, dribbling, etc. when a scrimmage is what he really wanted to do.

This leads us rather naturally to another essential consideration in carrying on an instructional lesson. The student must sense *the importance of what is to be learned*—importance to *him*. An instructor, in any subject area, at times finds this a real challenge. It does not usually suffice to speak of what is to be learned as being important for some future time. To inform a student that, unless this or that is learned now, he may not be prepared to support a family at some future time will not appear very relevant to him as an elementary school student. To the extent that the instructor can possibly do so, he must get the student to admit that "this, I'm encouraged to learn, is important to me at this time." To do so will tax the best an instructor possesses regardless of the content area in which he is assigned to give instruction.

A third consideration in an effective lesson is to *illustrate the effective use of the knowledge or skill* in situations understandable to the student. It is at this point that the instructor will reveal the preparation he has made for the specific student or group he is instructing. The instructor's choice of setting and instructional aids (see Chapter Seven) to be used will play an important role in whether what is to be gained from the lesson is understood. The instructor must know a great deal about his students in order to choose just how he can best bring about the desired result from a specific lesson—lecture, demonstration, field trip, or whatever one of a combination of activities.

Filtered through a lesson period there must be deliberate ways of *determining if understanding is developing* in the students. This becomes the fourth concern of the instructor—is understanding developing? This concern is not to be confused with testing for understanding at this point. Through observation and effective questioning and discussion, the instructor will be able to sense that understanding is or is not developing. Limited understanding or misconceptions are noted, and an attempt to clarify them through selected means is employed, keeping each student in mind.

Now it is time to *initiate the application of what has been gained* from the particular lesson, remembering the purpose is *not* to test but to afford a time for determining the need for more instruction or, perhaps, for modified instruction even more suited to an individual's needs. For an example, it is here that the use of workbooks, worksheets, or practice exercises can be effectively employed. The student applies specific learning in a controlled situation. He has an inherent right to expect immediate reinforcement from his attempt in the form of recognized success or promise of further instruction as the situation may call for. Conclusions about the student are not drawn; he is not pigeonholed as a success or a failure at this point. What is revealed is the necessity for more or less intensive instruction for each student relative to the objective of the lesson. Such action calls upon the greatest resources and, yes, patience of the instructor. What is planned at this time for further instruction for each student emerges logically from this present lesson.

Much like a research study in which certain variables are strictly controlled so that conclusions can be drawn from initiating other variables in a given situation, so should an instructor plan for the presentation of a specific lesson. The *setting of a lesson*, then, is a sixth major concern. By setting, reference is being made to the fact that literally all conditions are such that the challenge of the lesson can be focused precisely on what is to be learned. No part of the lesson situation will act as a barrier to the learning objective of the specific lesson—for example, (1) the printed context in which a new term is being introduced, (2) a skill that can be built directly from what a student now has under control, (3) an extension of a concept already initially well established with a student. If such a situation has been well planned, no need will reveal itself that will tend to distract from the task at hand. The common situation here is that the student possesses "readiness" for what is hoped to be accomplished in the lesson period.

Absent from a lesson period should be *the presence of threat* to the student. This suggests a seventh major concern—one that should permeate an instructional lesson period. Any feeling of threat on the part of a student can affect negatively what is planned to be accomplished in a lesson period. The writer has observed, and without a doubt has been responsible for creating, situations in a lesson period originally designed for instruction, where threat was obviously present. Observed were question sessions where questions were asked in such a way that students felt threatened. Teachers have been observed holding an open grade book while instruction was supposedly taking place. Students have often been prematurely cut off in their contributions without adequate time to develop the relationship they felt the contribution had to the topic under discussion. A different way of pursuing an answer to a problem has often been deemed unsatisfactory by a teacher. Sarcastic remarks by a teacher directed to specific students often terminate what might have proven to be a fruitful session of learning or clarification. It is the free "give and take," holding such within reasonable bounds, that diminishes the possibility of threat and should consequently lead to greater effectiveness of a given lesson.

## SUMMARY

In this chapter, several purposes for which instructional periods might be used have been considered. A number of factors relative to the assignment-making, guided study, presentation of content, stimulating discussion, and evaluating and measuring learning were discussed. In addition, suggested criteria in presenting a lesson were delineated. The importance of maintaining a threat-free teaching-learning environment, the value of providing specific objectives and purposes for a learner, and the necessity to adjust both presentation of content and assignments to accommodate individual differences in learners were pointed out as factors crucial to the attaining of effective subject-matter teaching and learning.

## QUESTIONS

1. Why is instructional time considered to be such an important segment of the school day?
2. Suggest and prepare to discuss instructional-time activities that should result in more thorough comprehension of subject matter.
3. What is the significance of the question: Are you chiefly a teacher or a tester?

*CHAPTER SEVEN*

# Utilizing Other Learning Aids

A student often lacks the experiential background necessary to enable him to cope with the knowledge, procedures, and skills required for understanding what is expected of him in a subject-matter area. For a student to make initial contact with subject matter at an abstract level such as the printed word is often a frustrating and unproductive experience. As efficient as the printed word can be for communicating ideas among those capable of understanding it, it can only be an effective medium when persons using it possess sufficient experience of a concrete nature that puts substance into the printed word for them. This chapter will point up considerations to be given the learning aids that can help prepare a person to carry on communication about subject matter at the abstract level through the medium of the printed word.

A statement long in use in educational circles is: "Experience is the best teacher." Perhaps this is true, but it must be realized that experience can be had in many forms, ranging from very concrete to very abstract. For one person faced with a learning situation, an experience which is abstract in nature may be very suitable. Another person faced with the same or similar learning situation may require a learning experience that

## 100 Utilizing Other Learning Aids

is far more concrete in form in order for him to develop an adequate understanding. It is essential, for effective learning to take place, that one or a combination of the appropriate experiences be made available to the learner to assure his adequate understanding of a subject-matter topic.

A teacher employed in a teaching-learning situation where facilities and materials and the time to utilize them effectively are available is professionally bound to select with care and use with discretion the instructional experiences deemed most suitable for the learner. Often, there is a temptation to assign virtually all learning to be obtained through the most common and available source—the textbook. Instead of yielding to this temptation, an effective teacher must, rather, consider the use of those learning experiences that most closely match the immediate needs and abilities of the learner at any specific time. To do otherwise might result in a lack of understanding of something considered to be of great importance. Later, upon the establishment of a foundation of experience, the learner may be able to add to his basic understanding by utilizing fewer and fewer concrete experiences, moving eventually to the printed page to further his understanding of a subject topic.

To make the preceding point clearer, consider the following example:

> A student has developed a curiosity and considerable interest in photography. He admittedly knows little about cameras, how to compose a picture, how to expose a film, how to develop the film, or how to make a print of the picture he has photographed.

For a person at this stage, very little might be gained initially through an attempt to get involved in photography through merely reading about the subject. There is surely a less abstract point at which he might enter the subject, one from which he might branch to a more thorough understanding and from which he could build proficiency in the execution of the act. An effective teacher would seek to determine the extent of the knowledge of photography that such a student possesses and would then provide sequentially the experiences—some more concrete, some more vicarious—that would effectively further the understanding and proficiency of the student in the art of photography.

The remainder of this chapter will present a point of view toward the use of instructional aids to learning that are, by nature, less abstract then the printed word, but which should eventually enable a person to gain more about a subject through the printed word.

A few decades ago Dr. Edgar Dale of Ohio State University prepared a chart in which various categories of learning experiences were arranged

Utilizing Other Learning Aids 101

from the most concrete in nature to the most abstract in nature. He labeled this chart the "Cone of Experience." Since then, thousands of teachers have used their interpretation of the chart in attempting to utilize a whole host of instructional materials and experiences to make the teaching-learning situation more effective. How would you interpret the chart and use its implications to improve the instruction of students in the content fields?

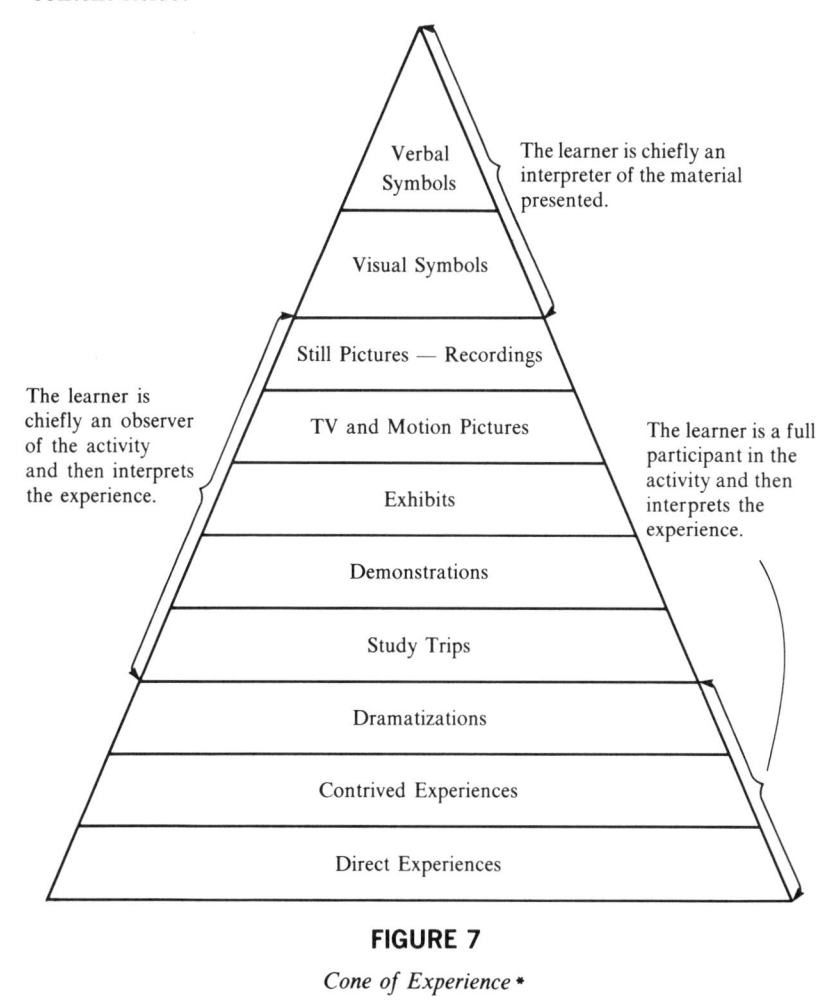

```
                    /\
                   /  \
                  / Verbal \     The learner is chiefly an
                 / Symbols  \    interpreter of the material
                /_____\   presented.
               /              \
              / Visual Symbols  \
             /_____\
            /                      \
           / Still Pictures — Recordings \
          /_____\
         /                                  \
The learner is    / TV and Motion Pictures \    The learner is a full
chiefly an observer                              participant in the
of the activity  /_____\   activity and then
and then interprets /                        \  interprets the
the experience.   /        Exhibits           \ experience.
                 /_____\
                /                                \
               /         Demonstrations           \
              /_____\
             /                                      \
            /            Study Trips                 \
           /_____\
          /                                            \
         /            Dramatizations                    \
        /_____\
       /                                                  \
      /           Contrived Experiences                    \
     /_____\
    /                                                        \
   /              Direct Experiences                          \
  /_____\
```

**FIGURE 7**

*Cone of Experience* *

---

*Adapted from Edgar Dale, "Cone of Experience," in *Audiovisual Methods in Teaching*, 3rd ed. Egar Dale (New York: Holt, Rinehart, & Winston, Inc., 1969), p. 107.

## 102  Utilizing Other Learning Aids

If the word "experience" in the statement "Experience is the best teacher" is interpreted to mean direct and meaningful participation in the learning situation, then many things must be considered before the learner is exposed to such direct participation. The following examples should point up the importance of this caution:

1. *Developing the Concept of the Relationship of Size and Motion.* A learner is faced with gaining an understanding of what is meant by the rotation and revolution of the Earth.

2. *Distance between the Learner and the Phenomenon to be Learned.* A student wishes to experience the viewing of the launching of a space craft.

3. *The Thing to Be Learned Involves Excessive Expense and Is Fragile.* A student is assigned the task of becoming familiar with the delicate parts of an orchid.

4. *The Situation Involves Distance and Lack of Experience.* A student is encouraged to develop an appreciation of the conditions under which children grow up in a ghetto area of an urban community.

5. *The Learner Faces a Time Differential.* A student is motivated to sense the intensity of the occasion of the signing of the Declaration of Independence.

6. *The Student is Required to Familiarize Himself with a Process.* A student is expected to know the process by which crude oil is refined to produce gasoline.

7. *The Learner is Faced with a Geometric Theorem to Be Understood and Applied.* A student is required to know that the square of the hypotenuse of a right triangle is equal to the sum of the squares of the other two sides of the triangle.

8. *The Learner is Expected to Develop a Manual Skill.* A student is required to produce a piece of furniture, using the various devices normally supplied in a wood-working shop, from a piece of expensive rough lumber.

9. *The Learner Faces a Geographical and Time Differential.* A student is

expected to appreciate the ordeals our ancestors endured in settling the western plains area of the United States.

At first glance, a direct, meaningful experience with a learning situation seems the perfect opportunity. However, a realistic consideration of many learning situations will make evident their impracticality or even their impossibility. Consider example number 2, *Distance between the Learner and the Phenomenon to be Learned;* how many learners could travel to and be accommodated at the site of a space ship being launched? Distance, expense, and appropriate use of time all enter the picture of this learning experience. In example number 3, *The Thing to Be Learned Involves Excessive Expense and Is Fragile,* the cost of providing such an expensive flower for every learner, along with its delicateness, precludes direct experiences. Example number 5, *The Learner Faces a Time Differential,* treats an experience completely out of the historical setting in which it occurred. Example 7, *The Learner Is Faced with a Geometric Theorem to Be Understood and Applied,* may appear impractical only because the instructor has been too short-sighted to realize the importance of a concrete illustration of a concept to be developed, while in example 8, *The Learner is Expected to Develop a Manual Skill,* it would normally be too dangerous and possibly too expensive to set the learner, in his initial experience, to the task of using a lathe, a planer, and other such tools with expensive rough wood.

In each example, the learning situation would surely need to be modified to make it most suitable for the learner. The direct, meaningful experience may be extremely unsuitable for the learner for varied reasons, including time, distance, danger, expense, and others. However, when the opportunity appears to be right for the learner, the instructional experience should be as direct and meaningful as possible.

Many instructional settings must be contrived in order to initiate effective learning and develop understanding. The real thing or event is often too overwhelming for the learner to grasp. For example, how can a finite person grasp the concept of the Earth's rotation and/or revolution (example number 1) by stepping outside and observing the relatively huge Earth in these movements? It is apparent that a model of the solar system used and demonstrated by the hands of a skillful teacher may be a better way to initiate the understanding of these movements of the Earth. A student could then explain why the sun appears in a different position in the sky hour by hour and season by season. Later, when the words *rotation* and *revolution* are used in printed material in reference to the movements of the Earth, it seems likely that a student will be better able to make sense about what he is reading. Many learning situations call for the instructor to use some contrived device (a model, a mock-up, or a process) in an attempt to establish more clearly a desired concept. In the majority of such situations the learner himself can manipulate these devices, permitting him to learn in what is very closely related to a direct, meaningful situation which is, nevertheless, controlled to avoid the drawbacks of the direct experience.

When a learner tries to recapture the feelings that might have permeated a group of people at the time a significant event occurred, he is often at a loss to do so. It is here that a form of dramatization—role-playing, for example—might assist in creating the desired emotional atmosphere. Example number 5 might call for just such a treatment. Would the statements purported to have been said by the participants in the event now quoted by present-day learners in a role-playing setting be likely to stimulate a little of the emotional feelings that existed at the time of the actual event?

Direct experience, contrived experiences, and forms of dramatizations all call for the learner to participate mentally, emotionally, and physically in the instructional experience. Virtually his whole being is employed in the process of gaining understanding. It seems advisable for the instructor to utilize to as great an extent as possible such instructional experiences as these in attempting to develop understanding in the subject areas. How much more meaningful will references to such subject topics be when met later in printed discourse.

There are a number of instructional experiences in which the learner is chiefly an observer of events through which he attempts to gain understanding rather than being a participant in a direct, contrived, or dramatizing way. In these instructional settings, the learner uses his ability to see and hear and, to some extent, his senses of smell, touch, and taste to gain the desired understanding. The learner uses his senses in a way that eliminates the barriers or dangers of the more direct, concrete experiences.

The field trip falls into this category. Here the learner is brought into the environment where the actual event is taking place. Under ideal conditions, the learner is in a position to observe what others may be in the act of doing. He can learn in the environment of real events, human or natural, utilizing his ability to see and hear with understanding.

The demonstration is, in a sense, a form of controlled field trip. The learner is still the observer; the demonstrator controls the experience provided. The demonstrator is in a position to manipulate the phenomena in order to present them to the best advantage of the learner. Example number 8 represents a situation that would lend itself early to the use of the demonstration. A trained teacher, capable of using a lathe with precision and safety, would demonstrate its use for the unskilled learner, who, in turn, through a step by step guidance program, gains the skill of using the lathe.

A less concrete but effective learning opportunity is the use of the exhibit. The exhibit presents an arrangement of materials in an order that permits learning from that order. Only a small part of the world's collections are ever arranged in such a way that learning can be gained by the observer. An exhibit is the result of order being made from collections. Specific items have been arranged by the expert so that the observer can learn from seeing and studying the exhibit. Museums, natural and industrial, are designed to present exhibits to the observer. Little does the casual observer realize the extent of the selection process that has gone on which resulted in the final exhibit. Many rather complex phenomena, processes, and settings have been made clear to the learner through the medium of an exhibit. The learner is an observer; yet, what he observes is an arrangement of the real or near-real that aids him in understanding. Some exhibits can be manipulated by the observer so that, through one or multiple cycles, a concept can be established about a given phenomenon. Example number 6 suggests a situation that might be successfully grasped through the medium of the exhibit.

The television and the motion picture media can present the learner with valuable learning experiences. Although considerably more abstract and remote than previously discussed experiences, television and motion pictures can stimulate the learner to use his eyes and ears acutely to glean understanding from these media. In fact these media, through special devices and effects, can improve on the direct experience even if it was available. The use of special lenses and stop-action photography are examples of this. Television is considered a bit more concrete than the motion picture chiefly because of the possibility it has to present to the learner a "live" situation. The motion picture is always a past account of an event. But both television and the motion picture call upon the learner to use his ability to see and hear as he attempts to gain understanding. A purposeful reason for viewing either a television or motion picture production is the possibility that a concept may be made clear at a time when such wouldn't be possible through printed material. Later, reading about the topic, previously introduced through television or the motion picture, may prove to be a rewarding and advancing experience.

Some learning experiences, unless purposely used in conjunction with each other, may stimulate learning through the use of only a single sense. The various forms of still pictures or sound recordings, although

## 106 Utilizing Other Learning Aids

less concrete than many learning experiences, are yet more concrete than language itself. The experience the learner may obtain from either of these forms or through the senses of touch, smell, or taste may well enhance his understanding of some topic he later has an opportunity to experience through printed language.

There is another category of experiences, quite abstract, yet less so than the printed word once learned. We are here referring to abstract symbols used on maps, diagrams, and in mathematical formulas—once learned, these symbols can stimulate almost immediate response and understanding for they leave less room for misinterpretation than the printed word. How do you respond to the symbols that follow?

When a learner has the background, built up through multiple contacts with the more concrete kinds of experiences, he should be far more able to handle with understanding topics he desires to pursue through reading from materials presented to him in print. Never is learning expected to be gained through only one medium of communication, for it is common for printed material to be infiltrated with the less abstract media for learning. It is the complementary use of these media at strategic times that tends to insure adequate understanding of ideas, events, and processes thought to be of importance.

## SUMMARY

This chapter has stressed the importance of utilizing various instructional learning aids for concept development. The aids have been presented in the chapter, beginning with those that are most concrete in nature through those that are more and more abstract. The teacher is challenged to select with care the aids to use relative to the needs of the student. The background provided through the use of well-selected aids will enable the student to better comprehend the subject matter he meets in printed form.

## QUESTIONS

1. Why is the printed word often the inappropriate resource to use in initiating the learning of subject matter?
2. How can a teacher determine the appropriate learning aids to use in developing subject-matter concepts?
3. In what types of situations would it be more beneficial to use a variety of learning aids rather than just one in developing subject-matter concepts?

*APPENDIX A*

# Answers to "A Subject-Matter Test"

1. A. a. It would be safest to buy two apple trees. Although many commercial apples are self-fruitful (i.e., a single tree can produce fruit), they do better with cross-pollination. In many cases, two different varieties of apples have to be planted together, but even when this is done, exceptions arise. For example, varieties such as Winesap and Rhode Island Greening cannot be successfully used together.
   b. One could buy a single peach tree if he used the proper variety; however, some varieties, such as J. H. Hale and Early Elberta, must be planted in groups of at least two trees.
   c. Again, if the proper varieties are used, one tree of each kind could be purchased and a harvest of fruit would be possible.
   B. Most states publish guides which are available from the state agricultural research office (e.g., *A Guide to Growing Fruit in Colorado.* Fort Collins, Colorado: Agricultural Experiment Station, Extension Bulletin 447 A).
   C. Within a source, "pollination" would be an appropriate entry to consult.

## 110  Answers to "A Subject-Matter Test"

2. A. A horizontal centrifugal pump—single stage.

   B. The state agricultural office or the U. S. Department of Agriculture. For example, some typical sources available from these agencies are listed below:

   *Equipping a Small Irrigation Pumping Plant.* Fort Collins, Colorado: Agricultural Experiment Station Bulletin 433.

   *Water: Yearbook of Agriculture, 1955.* Washington, D. C.: U. S. Department of Agriculture, 1955.

   C. "Irrigation" or "Pumps."

3. A. The correct answer is (b). The presence of bentonite is a cause for concern. There are two main varieties of bentonite. One is highly plastic and swells greatly as it absorbs water. Other clays that are called bentonite have quite different properties. The thickness of the bed might be a factor also. The state highway commission or state geological survey could help, once specific data were obtained on the chemical nature of the clay. The most plastic variety has high resistance to penetration. A modest house would probably have no problems, but one should check with experts before erecting a two-story brick structure or a house with a basement, since bentonite can shift and cause a cracking of the foundation.

   B. An encyclopedia.

4. A. The degeneration of the teeth, the attenuation of vision, and the diminishing of the sense of hearing as well as the loss of full power of other parts of the body is predicted. The reader is admonished to acknowledge the Creator while he enjoys the blessings of youth.

   B. A Concordance to the Bible.

   C. Yes. The presence of an ellipsis indicates an omission.

   D. Yes.

   E. A Bible commentary.

5. A. American Federation of Labor-Congress of Industrial Organizations.

   B. An almanac.

   C. An almanac.

## Answers to "A Subject-Matter Test"

6. B. An encyclopedia.

7. A. $11.33 for thirty days [interpolated from John E. Coffin, *Coffin's Interest Tables* (Philadelphia: John C. Winston Co., 1953)].

   B. No.

   C. *Coffin's Interest Tables* or a business handbook, such as *Financial Handbook*, ed. Jules Bogen (New York: The Ronald Press 1964) or *Handbook of Business Mathematics,* ed. William R. Minrath (Princeton: Van Nostrand, 1959).

8. A. "The filister head (machine screw) has a rounded top surface, cylindrical sides and flat bearing surface." [*Machinery's Handbook,* ed. Holbrook L. Horton, 17th ed (New York: The Industrial Press, 1964), p. 1080.]

   B. *Machinery's Handbook.*

9. A. A "French seam" is a special seam used especially for dainty baby garments and delicate lingerie. Its advantage is that it leaves no raw edges exposed.

   B. A book of the "handbook" or "guidebook" or "essentials" type. For example, Marjorie East and Mary E. Wines, *Fashion Your Own: A Guide to Easy Clothing Construction,* ed. Lela O'Toole (Boston: Houghton Mifflin Co., 1964).

10. A. Manitoba, Saskatchewan, or Alberta.

    B. The index.

    C. "Rape," "agricultural products," "field crops," or a similar entry.

    D. 123–25.

*APPENDIX B*

# Types of Word Pronunciation Errors: The IRI

## Error Of:

1. *Substitution:*    Occurs when a reader substitutes one or more words for another word or words.

2. *Mispronunciation:*    Occurs when a reader mispronounces a word.

3. *Refusal:*    Occurs when a reader cannot pronounce a word. The reader is allowed only five seconds to pronounce any given word. After a five-second interval, the teacher pronounces the word for the reader.

4. *Disregard of punctuation:*

5. *Omission:*    Occurs when a reader omits one or more words.

6. *Insertion:*    Occurs when a reader adds a word or words which are not present in the text.

## Additional Considerations

1. Only one error at any place in the reading is counted. Thus, if a reader substitutes a word and then repeats what he has read to correct his error of substitution, the error is counted as either an error of substitution or an error of repetition but *not* as both an error of substitution and an error of repetition.
2. An omission of two or three words in a row would be counted as only one error.
3. In basic sight word substitution, however, it is suggested that the teacher count such an error each time it occurs, since this type of error indicates that the reader cannot use the context of what he is reading in a meaningful way.
4. Mispronunciations of proper nouns or foreign words are not counted as errors, since decoding skills frequently have limited applicability to proper nouns or foreign words.

*APPENDIX C*

# Sources For Media Materials

*A Basic Book Collection for Elementary Grades*, 7th ed., American Library Association, 1970.

*A Multimedia Approach to Children's Literature*, American Library Association, 1972.

*Audio Visual Market Place*, R.R. Bowker Co., 1970.

*Book Selection Media*, National Council of Teachers of English rev. ed., 1967.

*Books for Children*, American Library Association, 1971.

*Educator's Guide to Free Films* (32nd annual), Educator's Progress Service, Inc., 1972.

*Educator's Guide to Free Filmstrips* (24th annual), Educator's Progress Service, Inc., 1972.

*Educator's Guide to Free Guidance Materials* (11th annual), Educator's Progress Service, Inc., 1972.

*Educator's Guide to Free Health, Physical Education, Recreation Materials*, Educator's Progress Service, Inc., 1971.

*Educator's Guide to Free Science Materials* (13th annual), Educator's Progress Service, Inc., 1972.

## Sources for Media Materials

*Educator's Guide to Free Social Studies Materials* (12th annual), Educator's Progress Service, Inc., 1972.

*Educator's Guide to Free Tapes, Scripts, and Transcripts* (19th annual), Educator's Progress Service, Inc., 1972.

*Educator's Guide to Free Teaching Aids*, Educator's Progress Service, Inc., 1971.

*Elementary Teacher's Guide to Free Curriculum Materials* (29th annual), Educator's Progress Service, Inc., 1972.

*Free and Inexpensive Learning Materials*, Peabody College-Tennessee, 1970.

*Index to Educational Audio Tapes*, NICEM, 1972.

*Index to Educational Records*, NICEM, 1973.

*Index to Overhead Transparencies*, R.R. Bowker, 1969-1973.

*Index to Producers and Distributors*, R.R. Bowker, 1973.

*Index to 8mm Motion Cartridges*, R.R. Bowker, 1969.

*Index to 16mm Educational Films*, R.R. Bowker, 1969.

*Index to 16mm Educational Films* (vol. I, II, III), University of Southern California NICEM, 1973.

*Index to 35mm Educational Filmstrips*, R.R. Bowker, 1970.

*Index to 35mm Filmstrip* (vol. I & II), R.R. Bowker, 1973.

*Learning Directory* (vol. 1-7), Westinghouse Learning Corp., 1970-71.

*Mountain Plains Film Catalog*, Mountain Plains—Educational Media Council, 1969-71.

*Mountain Plains Film Catalog*, Mountain Plains—Educational Media Council, 1971-73.

*Non-book Materials*, Canadian Library Association, 1971.

*Subject Index to Books for Primary Grades* (3rd ed.), American Library Association, 1967.

*Textbooks in Print including Related Teaching Materials*, R.R. Bowker, 1967 & 1968, 1972 & 1970.

*APPENDIX D*

# Suggested Readings

Burron, Arnold, and Claybaugh, Amos L. *Basic Concepts in Reading Instruction: A Programmed Approach.* Columbus, Ohio: Charles E. Merrill Publishing Company, 1972.

Culhane, Joseph W. "Cloze Procedures and Comprehension" *The Reading Teacher* 23, 5 (February 1970).

Dale, Edgar. *Audiovisual Methods in Teaching,* 3rd rev. ed. San Francisco: The Dryden Press, 1969.

De Chant, Emerald V. *Improving the Teaching of Reading.* Englewood Cliffs, New Jersey: Prentice-Hall, Inc., 1964. Chapter 13.

Durrell, Donald D. *Improving Reading Instruction.* New York: Harcourt Brace Jovanovich, 1956. Chapter 13.

Fry, Edward. "A Readability Formula That Saves Time." *Journal of Reading.* (April 1968).

Harris, Albert J., and Sipay, Edward R. *Effective Teaching of Reading,* 2d ed. New York: David McKay Co., 1971. Chapter 12.

Harris, Larry A., and Smith, Carl B. *Reading Instruction through Diagnostic Teaching.* New York: Holt, Rinehart, & Winston, Inc., 1972. Chapters 15 and 16.

## Suggested Readings

Heilman, Arthur W. *Principles and Practices of Teaching Reading,* 3rd. ed. Columbus, Ohio: Charles E. Merrill Publishing Company, 1972.

Karlin, Robert. *Teaching Elementary Reading,* New York: Harcourt, Brace, Janovich, 1971. Chapter 7.

Laffey, James L., editor. *Reading in the Content Areas.* Newark, Delaware: International Reading Association, 1971.

McCracken, Robert A. "Standardized Reading Tests and Informal Inventories." *Education* 82 (February 1962).

McKee, Paul. *Reading: A Program of Instruction for the Elementary School.* Boston: Houghton Mifflin Co., 1966. Chapter 9.

Miller, Wilma H. *The First R: Elementary Reading Today.* New York: Holt, Rinehart, & Winston, 1972. Chapters 13 and 14.

Smith, Nila Banton. *Reading Instruction for Today's Children.* Englewood Cliffs, New Jersey: Prentice-Hall, Inc., 1963. Chapter 10.

Wiechelman, Duane S. "A Comparison of Cloze Procedure Scores and Informal Reading Inventory Results." Doctoral dissertation, University of Northern Colorado, 1971.

Zintz, Miles V. *The Reading Process.* Dubuque, Iowa: William C. Brown Publishers, 1970. Chapters 9, 10, and 12.

# Index

Assessment:
  of students, 37-57, 69, 83, 85, 91-92
  of textbooks, 7, 59-63, 69
Assignment making, 25, 26, 27, 29, 30, 32, 34, 39, 48, 57, 69, 74-82, 83, 84-85, 98

Background (see Experience)
Barnes, Gail, 62
Burron, Arnold H., 50, 74

Capacity level, 38
Christenson, Adolph, 74
Claybaugh, Amos L., 50
Cloze test procedure, 49-53, 56
Comprehension, reading, 19, 43, 44, 45, 46, 78
Culhane, Joseph W., 50

Errors, in reading, 111
Evaluation (see Study Skills and Assessment)
Experience
  background of, 13, 18, 20, 27, 28, 74, 76-77, 82, 97, 100
  Cone of, 99-100
  variety of, 99-104

Farr, Roger D., 53
Frustration reading level, 38, 39-40, 44, 45, 46, 47, 51

Fry, Edward, 62
Functional reading levels, 38-49, 50, 73, 77

Graphic aids, 15, 19, 23, 49, 61

Heilman, Arthur W., 54

Independent reading level, 38, 39, 44, 45, 46, 47, 51, 74
Individualization of instruction, 7, 72, 69-73
Informal Reading Inventory (see Tests)
Instructional reading level, 38, 39, 44, 45, 46, 47, 51, 74
Instructional time, use of, 7
Interest, 15, 19, 74-76, 82
Italics (see Typographical cues)

Learning aids, 7, 33, 39, 66, 88, 93, 97-105
Library skills, 24-25
Location skills (see Study Skills)
Location test (see Tests)

McCracken, Robert A., 53
Motivation, 39 (see also Interest)

## Index

Pavlik, Robert, 60
Presentation of content, 87, 92-95:
  demonstration, 88, 93, 102
  discussion, 83, 89-91
  field trips, 88, 93, 102
  lecture, 89, 93
Purposes for reading, 79-80

Readability, 40, 62-63, 67, 68, 73, 74, 80, 85
Reference sources:
  almanac, 65
  appendixes, 23
  atlas, 25, 27
  card catalog, 24-25
  encyclopedia, 23, 27, 65
  graphic aids, 15, 19, 23, 49, 61
  index, 23, 55
  magazines, 23
  newspapers, 23, 25, 27, 66
  preface, 23
  *Readers Guide*, 25, 26
  tables, 23
  textbooks, 7, 23, 26, 27, 28, 54, 59-67, 71, 80-81, 82, 88, 91
  title, 23, 33
  utilization of, 59, 63-67, 74, 80-81, 82
  *Who's Who*, 25
Retention (*see* Study Skills)

Skimming, 24
SQ3R, 33

Study, guided, 85, 95
Study skills, 5, 6, 7, 19, 22-34:
  evaluation, 19, 25-29, 34
  location, 19, 22-25, 34, 54, 65, 85, 86
  organization, 19, 29-32, 34
  previewing, 78
  retention, 19, 32-34
Style, 14-15, 18
Subject matter:
  content, 6
  reading skills, 6-7
  test of, 2-5
Subject-matter materials:
  difficulty of, 39
  in classroom use, 51, 53, 57, 71, 77-79
  manipulation of, 70, 71
  reading problems posed by, 6, 10, 13-19, 61, 76, 78
  supplementary, 39

Tests:
  cloze, 49-53, 56
  Informal Reading Inventory, 38-49, 56
  locational, 54-56
  standardized, 53
Typographical cues, 16

Vocabulary, 13-14, 18, 21, 77-78

Weichelman, Duane, S., 49